Alan Davies is a comedian,
starring in the hit BBC seri
appearances as a panellist on *QI*.

'A simply astonishing achievement. The quality, depth, emotional power and terrifying honesty of Alan Davies's story-telling take the breath away. And what a story he has to tell. What a writer he is. Alternately funny, sad, frightening, sweet, savage and tender, *Just Ignore Him* will never leave you. I always knew that the dumb bewildered puppy persona that Alan so brilliantly projects was a mask for an acute, sensitive, powerfully intelligent and insightful mind, but nothing prepared me for such a tour de force of writing, for what is destined to become an instant classic. Not a klaxon but a peal of church bells and a twenty-one gun salute. Just Adore Him' Stephen Fry

'Tender, funny and unusually inspiring' David Sedaris

'One oft repeated speculation about comedians is that their "otherness", as children, led them to take on the mantle of class clown in order to deflect bullying. In truth, the reality is so much more difficult to unravel. In this book Alan Davies explores the complexity of events in his childhood whilst maintaining his trademark sardonic humour, warmth and intelligence. It's very, very sad at times, but a fascinating look at how childhood tragedy and trauma were treated in that era and how, leavened with humour, one individual/stand-up comic tries to make his way from the dark to the light' Jo Brand

'A heart-breaking but also uplifting memoir written with wit, wisdom and great humanity' Ben Elton

Just Ignore Him

Alan Davies

ABACUS

First published in Great Britain in 2020 by Little, Brown
This paperback edition published in 2021 by Abacus

1 3 5 7 9 10 8 6 4 2

A CIP catalogue record for this book
is available from the British Library.

ISBN 978-0-349-14436-8

Typeset in Caslon by M Rules
Printed and bound in Great Britain by Clays Ltd, Elcograf S.p.A.

Papers used by Abacus are from well-managed forests
and other responsible sources.

Abacus
An imprint of
Little, Brown Book Group
Carmelite House
50 Victoria Embankment
London EC4Y 0DZ

An Hachette UK Company
www.hachette.co.uk

www.littlebrown.co.uk

CONTENTS

Foundations   vii

Pictures   1

Tables   11

Fingers   21

Hands   27

Ashes   39

Gardens   55

Lanterns   65

Scales   75

Cigarettes   83

Animals   97

Pants   103

Exams   115

Beds   129

Housekeepers   141

Coins   151

Stamps   163

Songs   179

Holes   187

Buses   199

Magazines   213

Jokes   225

Submissions   239

Doctors   259

Cards   269

Acknowledgements   273

An Introduction

Foundations

At Sunday School as a boy I saw a demonstration of the parable of the Wise and Foolish Builders from the Gospel of Matthew, in which one house is built on sand, and another on rock. This lesson came to mind when I was asked to write this introduction, and again each time I considered it. When one thought follows another there might be significance in the connection, but why this particular Sabbath from the early seventies?

Two large trays were set on a table before a downbeat huddle of children in misshapen home-knitted jumpers, ill-fitting dungarees, and flared corduroys, all sat on the wooden floor of St Mary's Church Hall in the collective fug of a community that bathed once a week and washed their hair in the bath water. We could see that one tray held a mound of sand, and that each supported an identical doll's house. It was basic but good enough for an audience raised on the rudimentary ingenuity of BBC television's *Why Don't You Just Switch Off Your Television Set and Go Out and Do Something Less Boring Instead?*.

The telling of the parable began and a watering can was soon tipped out over the house on sand. Sadly, our teacher had no sidekick to play the Fool. They could have taken it in turns to drench each other's houses, with the Fool having the worst foundations but all the best jokes. Such is life, we might have learned.

Gravity took hold as the house sank on one side and then slid to the edge of the tray. The one on rock, or possibly breezeblock, withstood its downpour and the lesson was complete. A warning about the perils of subsidence had sunk in, so to speak.

The forces of gravity are omitted from the Gospels so I hope it isn't disrespectful to mention their role here. I missed the metaphor that this extreme weather event represented the trials and tribulations of life, examples of which may include false accusations, bereavement, and the vexations of strangers, as specified by St John Chrysostom, the fourth century Archbishop of Constantinople. Here was an influential Christian orator who considered homosexuality a sin worse than murder, practised only by the insane, and as such bears some responsibility for untold vexation upon strangers for centuries to come.

The rock represented the strength that faith in the teachings of Jesus Christ might provide, but that was also lost on me. I took it as straightforward testimony to the importance of what we now call Risk Assessment. Still, I apply the parable, when pitching tents or laying down a picnic blanket, always alert to the lie of the land, if not to ant nests and cowpats.

When I sat down to write this I still couldn't understand what caused me to recall that Sunday, even though my early years were not ideal, and I was exposed to changeable meteorological conditions (a metaphor, you understand, for the trials and tribulations etc., etc.).

Perhaps it's that simple. The parable has stayed with me because I knew that my own foundations were unstable. Now we're here, together, I'm inclined to point out the sand between our toes.

Writing this book became a process of continual revelation as I realised that recollections set firmly in my mind were often wrong, such as the years in which my grandparents died. I carried on, because I felt there was something in me that was blocked up, or buried, and if I could scalpel it out I'd be free of it. Forever. It became more of an archaeological dig in the memory than surgery, because the growth was not operable. The condition was diffuse. I carried it in every molecule of my flesh and bones and in every thought and action, in my hunched, splay-footed walk, my lisping Essex accent, and my lack of belief in a God who might have sustained me if I'd listened to the teachings, instead of those wretchedly boring hymns.

I could not purify the events of my early years, only organise this facsimile of them. If I were a stately home (intriguing enough to catch the eye, but in need of maintenance with many hidden parts beyond repair) this would be the guidebook, telling you a bit about what you are looking at and how it arrived at the condition it's in. If I were an electrical appliance, this is the troubleshooting section of the manual.

It's your book to use as you see fit; prop up a table leg, soak up a spillage, start a bonfire, but I hope you'll want to know what happens in the end, before you find other uses for the paper it's written on. We can only be certain, after all, that we have each other's stories and just in case there is no Kingdom of Heaven we best make sure we don't carry too many burdens while we are here, and share our tales among ourselves.

Alan Davies
March 2020

Pictures

I'd been driving along country lanes for an hour. The area felt both familiar and unfamiliar. As if I'd forgotten it completely and yet could remember it all. I hadn't been out here since I was a boy, when I was concerned only about the next corner and the one after that, as if the future was something you could rush towards and the past could be left behind. Later, I imagined that the past is not behind us at all, but unseen beneath our feet. We are supported by it as we walk, sometimes balanced, sometimes not, and if we tried we could reach below to grasp the person we once were. It might even be possible to pull them up to join us. Now I wonder if our past is always nearby, and our future too, and if we look carefully we can see both. But who wants to look carefully? There's certainly no time for that when you're racing along and there are trees rushing past that you could reach out and touch.

Gripping the wheel with both hands, leaning forward in my seat, I'd expected to find a discreet place to pull over in five minutes. Lying next to me on the passenger seat was my father's porn collection in a cloth carrier bag. The face of the PG Tips monkey, printed on its outside, looked up at me, giving nothing away.

If I crashed into a tree and was trapped, needing to be cut free, lifted clear and laid on a stretcher, spark out or even dead, then this bag's contents could change my life for ever, posthumously or otherwise. Was it too much to hope that the monkey would somehow seal the bag before the emergency services arrived, or that he could switch the contents, by sleight of knitted paw? He always seemed to have more about him than a real chimp in his TV ads. But that would just be a fantasy to cling to, while being shoved into an ambulance by an underpaid paramedic (is it possible to overpay one, has that been tried?).

There was more farmland out here when I was a teenager in the early eighties, tearing around in my Mini, looking for places to do handbrake turns. Now most of the openings on the side of the road led to private residences, with cameras at the gate to scrutinise the postman, the Pilates instructor, the pool cleaner and the minicab driver bringing domestic staff from the station (on account). If I pulled into an entrance my face might appear on a wall-mounted hi-def screen, in a box-fresh kitchen full of chef's knives, as I rifled through old pornography like a furtive, greying pervert:

'There's a car blocking the gate. He's just sitting there. He hasn't pressed the buzzer . . . What's he looking at? He's got piles of pictures . . . OH MY GOD, the sick bastard. Are the kids upstairs? Dave, where are the kids? Get your cricket bat. DAVID?'

I found an empty field and stopped parallel to a five-bar gate, with another similar opening across the road, and the car settled into silence. The interior warmed rapidly, the cold air turned off with the engine. All the roadside bushes were in leaf and insects flew about chaotically, looking for wild flowers, or aphids, or whatever they look for. Some have a single month of life, just one sight of the moon. Perhaps it feels like our three score and ten, their thirty-day turd-hunt, that's if they're not eaten by a blackbird on day one, or splatted by a motorcyclist's visor on day two.

The sky was blue, dotted with white fluffy clouds. It would be nice to come back as a cloud, in the so-called next life. People go on about returning as cats, or lobsters, or Golden Eagles, no one ever says a cloud. Drifting along on the breeze, watching the cars, and the cows, and the crop circles, before falling exhilaratingly to earth, rushing together into a stream and then being spirited up again. That's a nice life, if you can avoid cisterns and urinals. It might even be pleasant to evaporate, a good way out. Maybe some water never disappears, stuck for ever in one existence. How awful.

I thought about walking across the field, leaving the gate and the car door hanging open, all the way to the other side, hopefully days away, mile after mile of dry, brown, knee-high grass, then pushing through a hedgerow into an unburdened life replete with new memories, no bad ones, and somehow knowing the way home.

Or the bad memories have sunk into a dank peat bog at the bottom of the brain where it's always night, the sun can't reach, and the learned lessons of life dissipate throughout the unwitting mind, into future behaviours, guiding us away from repeating errors, extinguishing the half-thrill that was part of a terrible time, so nothing appeals about returning, not even familiarity, and we learn but can't recall how. This better, evolved brain can filter memory, detect remnants of rage or trauma, and sink them in the brain-bog where they are only echoes of what to avoid.

I stayed in the car. The gate looked heavy and the cloud I envied had gone. I was in P for park. If there was no other life, before, during or after this, I needed to be ert not inert. I didn't want to check out.

A pristine white Range Rover Evoque appeared in my rear-view mirror, a fast-moving reminder that other people were out here, and this was not going to remain a private place. I sank into my second-hand car seat as this engineering marvel approached; it was over-equipped for this B road, but just the sort of vehicle you'd expect to see among all these large properties. Buying one is thriftless and I felt a pang of jealousy at the fearless spending it represented. The chucking away of money is beyond me, handicapped as I am by the pitiable passed-on characteristics of poor taste and bean-counting.

This is the true inheritance tax of life. Behaviours and habits, ingrained, your own but not your own, a duty on your existence, a tariff to be levied on those who try to love you.

As I waited for the Range Rover's windblast I held on to the monkey bag, with its envelope full of my dad's favourite photos. This was not an inheritance. It was contraband from a theft carried out by my stepmother. Dad had accrued this latest portfolio only after she had found one such image stuck fast in their home printer. He then admitted he had some similar items hidden in his built-in wardrobe. It turned out there were hundreds of pictures, which they had secretly burned in their back garden eight or nine years ago, when they were both in their seventies, shuffling about curiously in the night-time with a box of matches, making a pensioners' Pact of Fire, blackening the lawn beyond the crazy paving where a magnolia tree once stood, all in lieu of the torching of their suburban reputation.

Scorching that earth was an attempt to destroy clues to my father's hidden nature, a side of him that I did not know about, and that she made him promise would be discontinued as he begged her not to tell anyone. But Dad spoke with forked tongue in the powwow before the flames, when he said his downloading days were done, and he continued to press *print* whenever his wife was out of the house, *print, print, print, print, print (repeat)*.

It wouldn't be long before he noticed that this folder of pictures was missing. When I'd smuggled it out into my car he was carrying a jug across the patio, slowly, like a koala poisoned by eucalyptus, his old legs on show in old shorts, in order to pour water into a birdbath.

My stepmother had already described to me, over the phone, some of the people in the pictures, with safe-for-work descriptions of their activities, and chosen to confide that many of them looked like me. I'd insisted I wanted to see all of it, and told her not to burn anything else. My siblings already knew about this collection, but they hadn't seen it and wanted everything disposed of without looking. Their own status quo was good enough for them, and my stepmother too claimed she wanted it gone, but she had passed it on to me, so did she actually want everyone to know about it? Was I the sacrificial messenger?

She put the folder into the monkey bag to minimise the risk of the contents blowing all over the neighbours' block paving, as she played out a confused double game of revealing a hidden truth while trying to keep it a secret.

Now that the Evoque had gone and I was in peaceful solitude, among the birds and the bees, I didn't want to look in the bag. 'I don't think you'll like it,' my stepmother had said, but that wasn't what was stopping me. Taking this

step might shift too many supporting pillars in my emotional infrastructure, which already resembled a makeshift
shanty town put together after a hurricane, with psychological corrugated sheeting and unbalanced blue tarpaulins.
It lacked stability but it held, some new life had grown up
around it, there hadn't been a storm for a while and I didn't
want my shack of feelings blown down, like a little pig's in
a fairy tale.

I looked at the face of the knitted monkey, took a breath,
reached across and pulled out . . . my phone.

I typed *PG Tips* into the search bar.

Launched by the Brooke Bond Tea Company in 1930,
PG Tips was marketed as Pre-Gest-Tea, to be drunk before
meals to aid digestion. Such claims were subsequently out-
lawed but the PG brand remained and Tips was added in
reference to the part of the plant used. Dad loves tea, he
makes a sound of approval with every sip, but if he doesn't
have a teaspoon he'll say: 'I haven't got a *teaspoon*,' and my
stepmother will hurry in from the kitchen to find him one
in the sideboard, a few feet from his chair.

I put my phone down and looked in the bag. There was a
large manila envelope inside the folder and, having checked
my wing mirrors several times for dog walkers, I slid out the
contents. Now they were available to view, I stared through
the windscreen, down the long straight road ahead, where
some cyclists had appeared, four grown men in colourful
skin-tight outfits. It seemed unlikely that they were in a
race, more that they were pretending to be. They edged
nearer in their garish amateur peloton, but they were a long
way off, so I looked down at the first picture.

It featured a boy of about fifteen, wearing an unsmiling
expression and nothing else, kneeling on a bed looking

straight at the camera, playing up a little with a manufactured sneer. He was a pinkish white colour, his dark hair cut short, his chest pale, with little muscle definition or body fat, not skeletal but not yet full-grown. He was at rest. There was no fake tan or waxed skin, just moles and blotches. I looked around the edges of the image for any sign of the website it had come from. There was no clue as to who this kid was, or where the picture was taken, or whether the law would consider him a child.

Or whether his parents would.

I realised that the cyclists were seconds away. I'd forgotten them, and everything else, as I looked at the picture. They were fast, could it be the Essex Police Road Racing team on a training ride?

My window was down so I held the envelope and the photos against my chest, in case the slipstream from the peloton drew the pictures out to flutter across the countryside, some settling in hedges for schoolboys to find, others being snatched up by the gloved hand of a wannabe Bradley Wiggins. He'd look down at me across his handlebars, and I'd gaze up over his ventilated helmet, longing to be a cloud.

I turned away to avoid eye contact. They went past. A fly bonked into my windscreen. I looked at the next picture.

Two teenage boys this time, also naked and concentrating intently as they stared at the glans (from the Latin for acorn) of one as if it were independent of them both, in between them and readying to dock, like a shuttle nearing a space station.

This was not a well-lit photo and there was evidently no art department on hand to choose bedclothes. Again there was no indication of where or who they were, or whether they should have been at school that day. But this one bore a logo in the corner, *Teens*, a word now made ugly, a mask of everyday normality thrown over a private peepshow. The font was swirly and colourful as on a child's birthday card, with puffed-up letters squidging against one another.

Does my father become excited when he looks at these joyless images created in squalid polyester bedrooms for secretive voyeurs? What a misstep in life for all concerned.

The pictures piled up, all naked boys together. My stepmother said that they were 'vile', but they just seemed sad, with nothing tender to be seen, no warmth or affection. There were occasional shy smiles in some but in others no faces at all, just limbs, buttocks and cavities, a smear of something here and there, and graphics in the corner saying 'teen' or 'twink' or 'boy' in various bright and breezy typefaces usually reserved for children's television channels.

I looked down at the PG Tips monkey on the seat next to me and its eyes met mine as if to say: 'Do not implicate Unilever, my parent company, in this. They are a litigious multinational and will not take kindly to being depicted as the bearers of boy-cock action snaps, unknowing or otherwise, *capiche*, mister?'

His face bore no such warnings. Blank, expressionless, regarding everything and nothing, just like mine. Stuck fast in a new phase of my existence, no idea what to do. Inert.

There was movement outside the car. A farmer was striding towards me. There was a tractor waiting to go through the gate I was in front of. He looked amazed that anyone could be so adrift that they wouldn't notice his chugging power plant, his throbbing pipes, his flashing lamps.

'I'll move,' I said.

I didn't want him to come any closer.

'You can put it over there,' he said.

'It's okay, I'll move it!'

We were both shouting.

'You can park in that one!'

He was pointing at the entrance on the other side of the road. He had two cars behind him. I could see the faces of the drivers. I was clearly visible but I'd managed to hide the porn I'd been staring at, by an empty field, in the middle of the day.

I started the engine and surged alarmingly across the lane into the other entrance and then reversed without coming to a stop, before setting off the way I'd come, fighting the urge to accelerate up to eighty or ninety miles an hour. My dad liked to drive fast, he got me into cars. I could speed along until no one was behind me and then unseal the electric sunroof and lift the pictures clear of the opening into the wind before releasing them like a vapour trail of depravity, followed by the monkey.

But I didn't eject the evidence, because among all those images of boys, presumably taken by men, there were four photographs of a long-legged man in his forties. He was posing, not quite proudly, in tiny red briefs, as close to nude as he dared, given that the photos would have had to be developed at the chemist. In two of them he was standing, in a third he was on his haunches in a bathroom, trying to grin, now in tight blue undies, and in the fourth he was sitting on a sunny balcony, smiling happily, his pants now off and placed on his genitals, a turquoise blob of fabric.

Who had taken these holiday snaps? Or were they self-portraits done on a timer? Not that last one, I'd have thought. Who can run back into position before the view-finder, casually cross their legs in a spontaneous display of giddy relaxation, and then balance a screwed-up posing pouch atop their middle-aged cock and balls, all in ten seconds?

That turquoise was familiar, our windowsills were painted that colour at home when I was growing up, and I recognised the holidaymaker in the pictures too.

I'd seen him only recently, on his way to fill a birdbath.

Tables

Maybe my mother thought I was dead, since I wasn't responding to her cries. She came barrelling into the living room at top speed, wearing an anxious look I hadn't seen before. Crawling about beneath the table in the bay window, I'd become tangled among the gate-legs that pulled out either side to support a pair of drop leaves. As I bumped about, the vase on top fell over. A big, white, Art Deco thing, with bulging sides in sections, creating the impression of wavy lines going from top to bottom. Mum had put some flowers in it, yellow ones.

I was frozen in fear and looking at the doorway before she arrived, expecting to be in trouble, since she'd shouted and then come running. She was going to be cross about the vase, though I don't remember it being broken or even any water from the flowers dripping down. That I expected her concern to be the china, not me, might say something about how I saw myself in the household pecking order, aged three. Or it might mean I broke a lot of stuff and was used to people, not me, picking up the pieces. I do remember breaking a light fitting once, years later, but she was dead by then so I just lied about it to my dad, since he would be livid either way.

Maybe I had seen that anxious look on Mum's face

before, I don't remember, but it was an unexpected delight that she coaxed me out from under the table and hugged me, not even looking at the vase, comforting me when she realised I was frightened by the crash and the shout and the running and the thought that I'd broken something. Her relief flooded over me and, in the mysterious world of emotional alchemy, transformed inside me to joy.

That is a memory of love, I know what love feels like, it feels like that.

The main table in our house was not that gate-leg one in the window, with flowers from our garden sitting on top in a nice old vase, it was the dining table at the other end of our knocked-through downstairs rooms. The house was built in the thirties, a detached suburban home we'd moved to in 1968, in time for my sister to be born in the back bedroom that November. I don't know if she was there at the time of gate-leg-table-gate, if she wasn't then Mum might have been pregnant.

You could release a catch on either side of the dining table and pull the ends apart. A middle section would rise up, and unfold into the gap to make the table bigger if you had visitors. I don't remember the visitors.

It was an impressive sight, the emerging slab of timber, and there was an element of risk as a small child might stray underneath during the lifting. 'Mind your fingers' was a frequent cry in our house, usually in doorways but at the table too.

I have no memory of my mum at the dining-room table. This seems inconceivable. Where did she sit when we ate? I do remember her in her bedroom, attaching stockings to a girdle that looked like a parachute harness. Sitting at her dressing table, being called 'Darl' by my dad. I remember her in the kitchen, making jam, and then jam tarts, and letting me bang saucepan lids together like the man on the cymbals in *Trumpton*. I remember her putting me in the bath when I still had socks on, and how my laughing made her laugh. I remember a blue plastic bucket with a lid and before you got in the bath she would hold the lid upside down so you could do a little wee into it, which she would tip into the basin. Better that than weeing in the bath. I remember her reversing her black Morris Minor Traveller into a ditch outside infants' school and being inside the car while men pushed us back up on to Staples Road, which had Epping Forest running all down one side, and if we hadn't stopped we might have rolled all the way to Dick Turpin's old hideout, I imagined.

But I don't remember her at the dining table, though we must have had so many meals together, Sunday roasts and teatimes.

I don't remember a single breakfast with her.

All the times she tucked me in, all the stories she must have read, but I don't remember her in my bedroom.

I was nearly six and a half when she died. Six years, five months and sixteen days, in fact, or six years one hundred and sixty-nine days, or two thousand three hundred and sixty-one days (including the leap years of 1968 and 1972). She was born on February 5th 1934 and was thirty-eight when the leukaemia finished with her, so she would have been a white-haired old lady by now, if she'd lived, but she might have died another way, of course, a vase falling on her head or something.

I don't see the point of leukaemia. Some diseases are using you as the host for a time and then they transfer to someone else, they survive that way, those pathogens, airborne or waterborne, jumping from person to person or cow to cow or rabbit to rabbit. But leukaemia just sets up a malfunction in you that you can't survive. Nothing grows or thrives except tiny cell-size tumours inside your bones. No one knows what causes it. It's a genetic mutation that occurs when you're making jam or putting your kids in the bath. The advice is: don't smoke and eat more vegetables. That's the best they can offer, even now in 2020, never mind 1972. My mother did not smoke and was in the greengrocer's almost daily. What a pointless thing it is. And people say they don't understand why there are wasps.

It is thought that 90sr can cause that genetic mutation. It's a radioactive isotope of strontium produced by nuclear fission and is of concern in the event of nuclear fallout or leaks. 90sr is known as a Bone Seeker. As far as I know, the nearest nuclear power station to us was Sizewell on the Suffolk coast, eighty-eight miles away. It opened in April 1967, thirteen months after I was born. They have *nearly* had leaks, and some radioactive material has been found on Southwold beach, but I don't think we ever went there. Mum wasn't caught out by a Bone Seeker, she just mutated by herself, like the X-Men, and her white blood cells went on the rampage.

I do remember my dad at the dining-room table.

'Lay me half a table, would you?'

This meant putting a tablecloth halfway across, with a place mat (we had a set of six with cars on from the early twentieth century) and cutlery from the sideboard. He would then sit down with a boil in the bag chicken and mushroom casserole sloshed up next to some boiled (to submission) potatoes and frozen veg. If it was early enough he might watch *MASH*, and laugh at Hawkeye and Frank Burns, but usually he sat down in time for the *Nine O'Clock News* on the

BBC. This meant it was time for bed, from where you could hear him copying the impressionist Mike Yarwood's voice to mock the Labour Prime Minister Jim Callaghan:

'I'm going to be perfectly blunt,'

and the Labour Chancellor of the Exchequer, Denis Healey:

'What a silly billy.'

Dad venerated Sir Winston Churchill and purred reverently every time we passed his statue, in the neighbouring constituency that he used to represent.

The television was on a trolley so it could join us kids at the table at our earlier teatime, like the fourth sibling we all loved the most. We watched *Crackerjack*, *Rentaghost*, *Blue Peter* and *Grange Hill*, and just before the early news a final short children's programme like *The Magic Roundabout* or *Paddington*.

Then my brother would do his homework at the dining table. He wrote left-handed but curved his arm all the way around the top of the paper so his hand didn't smudge or obscure what he was writing. With his right hand he held a clear six-inch plastic ruler in his mouth. The end was mangled and coated in saliva. There were constant sucking and chewing sounds that went on all through *Nationwide* and were often still a distraction during *Terry and June* at seven o'clock.

During one session of bickering in the dining room my brother stood behind where I was sitting and held a glass ketchup bottle high up at arm's length, as if he were about to smash it on the back of my head. We agreed that if he did I would probably die. I told him I'd rather be dead than in prison, which was where he would be going. Then I waited for him to do it. I actually thought he might, but I wasn't going to move. I wondered if the glass would break and there would be red sauce everywhere. He said that it was 'so tempting', and I said, 'Go on then.'

It was a relief when he put the bottle down. I behaved like the victor for a while, as I was not dead, though in our house whether it was best to be dead or undead could be considered a moot point.

After Mum was gone Dad put a half-size snooker table next to the dining table, a competition-standard dartboard on the wall, and then, in a new extension at the back, a full-size table tennis table. On the other side of new plate-glass sliding doors was a paved area with a wall you could hit balls against, and up the garden, past the swing, was a badminton court marked out in whitewash on the lawn and finally a wooden goal net he'd had made, standing in front of Mum's rose bed.

He liked sport.

Despite his love of ballgames and motor racing, he did not download and print pictures of John Newcombe or Jimmy Greaves, or Denis Compton or Mike Hailwood, or any of his other heroes. I conclude that sport is his second favourite pastime.

When we played Trivial Pursuit at the dining table and he landed on Art & Literature, he'd groan and say: 'Oh no, *Aaarrt* and *Litch-ra-chure*', in a voice that told you that art or literature alone were boring but together they were so life-threateningly tedious he couldn't even speak properly.

In a glazed bookcase in my dad's bedroom were my mum's souvenir books from Shakespeare productions at the Old Vic, dating from the fifties. Large hardbacks in dust jackets, filled with black-and-white photos of the actors, among them the dreamy Richard Burton who had turned down a Hollywood contract in order to play Hamlet at the

Old Vic in 1953, when he was twenty-seven and Mum was nineteen. He also played Henry V, Othello, Caliban and Coriolanus, as well as Sir Toby Belch and Philip the Bastard. I'm not sure how many of those performances Mum saw but I remember my dad saying she went there, in his version of events, just to ogle Burton. I assume they didn't go together, given that he used to say '*Wich-ud Buurr-don*' in the same droning voice he used for Art & Literature.

Perhaps she went with her younger sister or friends from home or from work. Typing-pool girls and secretaries who would go into London by train, work all day and then stay on to see a show. Nowadays Mum might have gone to university, but I learned from her cousin Michael that she was told by my grandparents that she had to go out to work, to bring money in. Eventually these young women would marry, from home, and go straight to live with their husbands. They weren't so welcome in the workplace after that, and certainly once they'd had a baby they were never employed in a typing pool again. Mum could have gone somewhere to study Shakespeare, but maybe the sacrifices necessary for her parents to send her would have weighed too heavily, so she accepted her lot. Or perhaps it hurt her, to know that her intelligence and curiosity were to be curtailed before she even started.

She'd have been good at Art & Literature, and given short shrift to Dad's moaning. She loved Shakespeare, she loved Richard Burton and she loved me as well. So he hated Shakespeare, and Burton, and maybe he hated me sometimes, with my jaunty ways learned in her company as her little friend.

Perhaps Mum loving me bothered my brother, too. There's nothing to suggest she didn't love him, but one day, when he was two, he pulled my pram over when I was asleep in it. Another time, long after she was gone, I was sitting at the dining table while my brother was playing darts, and I managed to become so irritating that he threw a dart at me. He deliberately missed, opting for a shot across my bows, and the dart stuck in the carpet in front of the sofa. Foolishly, given he still had two darts in his hand, I mocked his aim and his inability to go through with his threat.

There were no darts thrown or bottles wielded over heads when Dad was at the table with us. When I was being annoying (not sure how, it just came naturally) he would turn to my brother and sister and say:

'Just ignore him.'

And they did. Dad chewed his food, with his cutlery resting on his plate and a solemn expression on his face, as the whole family watched *Grandstand* on a Saturday lunchtime. I would look at him, as he masticated faultlessly, knowing he could feel my gaze but wouldn't acknowledge it, and my brother and sister tuned in to his wavelength and so I learned that I was to blame for all the sadness, all the pain, all the aching emptiness everyone felt. It was down to me mucking about, not Mum dying, not the mutation.

It was tough to be ignored. I had to pretend that it wasn't so hurtful that I'd still be thinking about it forty years later. I'd chirrup away a bit longer to keep the silence at bay until my dad ended that with:

'If you haven't got anything nice to say, just say nothing.'

On one occasion I said:

'Nothing, nothing,

nothing, nothing, nothing, nothing, nothing, nothing,
nothing, nothing, nothing, nothing, nothing, nothing,
nothing, nothing, nothing, nothing, nothing, nothing,
nothing, nothing, nothing, nothing, nothing, nothing,
nothing, nothing, nothing, nothing, nothing, nothing,
nothing, nothing, nothing, nothing, nothing, nothing,
nothing, nothing, nothing, nothing, nothing, nothing,
nothing, nothing, nothing, nothing, nothing, nothing,
nothing, nothing, nothing, nothing, nothing, nothing,
nothing, nothing, nothing, nothing, nothing, nothing,
nothing, nothing, nothing, nothing, nothing, nothing,
nothing, nothing, nothing, nothing, nothing, nothing,
nothing, nothing, nothing, nothing, nothing, nothing,
nothing, nothing, nothing, nothing, nothing, nothing,
nothing, nothing, nothing, nothing, nothing, nothing,
nothing, (turn the page, there's nothing to see here),
nothing, nothing, nothing, nothing, nothing, nothing,
nothing, nothing, nothing, nothing, nothing, nothing,
nothing, nothing, nothing, nothing, nothing, nothing,
nothing, nothing, nothing, nothing, nothing, nothing,
nothing, nothing, nothing, nothing, nothing, nothing,
nothing, nothing, nothing, nothing, nothing, nothing,
nothing, nothing, nothing, nothing, nothing, nothing,
nothing, nothing, nothing, nothing, nothing, nothing,
nothing, nothing, nothing, nothing, nothing, nothing,
nothing, nothing, nothing, nothing, nothing, nothing,
nothing, nothing, nothing, nothing, nothing, nothing,
nothing, nothing, nothing, nothing, nothing, nothing,
nothing, nothing, nothing, nothing, nothing, nothing,
nothing, nothing, nothing, nothing, nothing, nothing,
nothing, nothing, nothing, nothing, nothing, nothing,

nothing.'

And they still ignored me, no one cracked, they sat at the table and stared at the television.

Could those bleak recollections of our dining table have overlaid memories of my mum, like the ash from Vesuvius that covered Pompeii?

I have fonder memories of the gate-leg table because of the love I felt under there, and I can bring those memories back because I'm writing this in my own house, sitting at that same table.

Fingers

Mum must have felt she couldn't turn her back on me, couldn't leave me alone for two minutes. If I wasn't bumping into furniture and knocking over vases then I was drinking detergent in the kitchen.

We still had an outside toilet and perhaps she'd just disappeared in there for a moment, out of the back door from the kitchen into the sideway, where a high fence of upright wooden planks separated us from the neighbours, then through a door in the side of the house with gaps at top and bottom. A string hung down to operate a bare light bulb. It was cold in there and three growths of fungus lived in the angle between the wall and the ceiling, curving out like the edges of different coloured dinner plates. I was told not to touch the fungi, even though I could never have stretched my little fingers right up there. We were also told not to touch any fungus in Epping Forest. A fear of poisoning had been instilled.

Where I could reach, aged about three, was up above my head to a green plastic cup on the draining board in our kitchen. I could only just hook two of my fingers through the handle. It wasn't my usual drinking cup, mine was orange, but it was identical otherwise and I lifted it down. There was a small amount of fluid in the bottom, not enough but I drank it all the same, expecting orange squash. It tasted wrong, I thought at first it was just undiluted, but then it was stinging and hostile and Mum was there, horrified, taking the cup away and asking me if I was all right and had I drunk any of it, as the detergent coated the inside of my throat. Perhaps she'd been washing something in the sink, out of my sight, and was using the cup to keep some sort of liquid soap in. It can't have been bleach, which would have stripped the taste buds off my tongue in seconds; it was more like washing-up liquid. Maybe she'd gone to a neighbour for a squirt of theirs, as she'd run out.

Should I drink water? Would I start to bubble and foam? Or was it better to rinse out, slosh around and spit, gargle, and spit some more? I looked at her with my mouth hanging open, tears everywhere, snot, panic, fear, a look that said:

'Will I ever be all right? Will I ever be the same again?'

And she looked at me, and her face said:

'Will you ever be all right? Will you ever be the same again?'

After more sluicing with tap water, my throat began to feel better. I stopped crying, she was looking at me; how nice to have the undivided attention of my mother. I don't think that's why I did it, although I had a baby sister to contend with by then so we can't rule it out. I think I was just thirsty. There was no ulterior motive at work, at least not consciously. It's an effective tactic for attention, drinking a domestic solvent, the house could have been flooding around us and Mum would still have been concerned about burns to my epiglottis, my soft palate, my trachea.

Afterwards I had some squash, in my own cup. I watched

her fingers turn the cold tap, and we were relieved that I hadn't died and a tiny bit of distance opened up between us, to be closed again at the next crisis.

If you wanted something to drink or to eat, or clothes to wear, or if you wanted to be put in the bath or helped on with your shoes, or if your homemade rabbit's ears needed fastening (very tight under the chin since they were too small), then it was Mum's fingers you needed. I watched those fingers all day long, her kneading and rolling of pastry, her peeling of potatoes, her donning of the oven gloves or the washing-up gloves or the gardening gloves. Those fingers were never in repose. They came at you with a hankie damp with saliva and cleaned round your mouth, they brushed your hair, rubbed a wet flannel over your face, pulled your mittens on string through your coat sleeves. They were snapping open the clasp on a handbag, snapping shut the clasp on a purse, twisting a lipstick, flipping open a compact and patting the inside with a pad, the wafting sweet smell of which is an olfactory memory I'd be afraid to be reminded of now, for fear of it being too sad to bear.

Her fingers lifted the lids on her Wedgwood pots, threaded needles and sewed name-tags into clothes. They pushed giant safety pins through terry-towelling nappies (am I remembering my own or my sister's?) and smaller pins into a pin cushion.

They filled shopping baskets, with meat wrapped in paper, a long tin loaf from the baker's and brown paper bags full of carrots and sprouts. They never boiled rice or stirred pasta, which Dad would not eat, they poured tea through a strainer, squeezed boiled fruit through muslin, whipped up egg whites for lemon meringue pie, lined cake tins, greased pans, stewed blackberries and apples, diced kidney into casseroles, chopped the fat off meat, chipped and fried or boiled and mashed potatoes, and placed fairy cakes in a line on a rack to cool before pulling the washing out of a top-loader with big wooden tongs.

They sliced bread, buttered crumpets, stirred soup and pulled the skin off rice puddings. They pushed the middle of the silver top down on the milk bottle to make a lid, then set the dial on the milk carrier to let the milkman know how many pints, please. They swept and wiped and wrung out, they ironed and folded and carried to the airing cupboard, they lowered boys one at a time into a bath a touch below scalding before bringing them out pink and scrubbed to be dried by those fingers cloaked in coloured towels, ready for clean white sheets, to be tucked in and to sleep soundly in a way that would never be possible when those fingers were gone.

Outside they snipped and pruned and tied back, they burrowed into the earth and settled new plants into beds, they eased weeds out by the root and held sweet peas to my nose so I could smile wide-eyed at their lovely scent. All the vulnerable little life forms she wanted to flourish and thrive did exactly that, prodded and pushed and watered and shown the sun, and when she was done she'd reach down and I'd reach up, my little fingers taking hold of one or two of hers instinctively, my arm rising as if gravity had let it go and our hands docking in silence, holding tightly, without thinking, fingers that belonged together.

And then indoors again those fingers would take my hand and two of them would walk on my palm, 'Round and round the garden like a teddy bear, one step', up my arm, 'two step', further up, 'and tickle you under there', and I would giggle and laugh and she might do it again, or tell me which little piggy went to market and which little piggy ran all the way home.

Ready to work, to do hundreds of things every day, those fingers, against their will, shrivel, weaken, can just place a pill on a tongue, slowly lift a glass to lips, they rest on the bed sheets, stilled by the body's effort to save strength, to stave off frailty, to last a little longer, waiting to reach out and touch her children, who she never slapped or smacked or gripped too firmly or shook or grabbed, and who won't now be brought to see her again, no more little fingers to reach out and marvel at, no scent of children, no stickiness, no grasping, nothing to hold as life slips out and poisoned blood rests still beneath those nails that plucked out tiny splinters. Then removed secretly by strangers to a wooden box and burned, not for fuel, not for warmth, only for convenience, scraped up and poured into a pot, put in the ground without a witness to mark the spot, never to be found, my ten little friends all gone.

Hands

My dad towered over me when I was a boy. He had a long and narrow trunk, topped with black foliage that was brushed down, parted, and held fast with Brylcreem. His hands were seemingly always by his sides, close to my head height. His tummy (never a stomach or a belly in our house) protruded, so he looked as though he was leaning back, giving an impression of arboreal hesitancy. I was a human epiphyte, a tolerated clinging dependant of no benefit to the host.

He was oddly flat-handed. Not in palms-up supplication, and not with unusually shaped hands like pancakes. They were lifeless, with the fingers extended, hanging down, not curled in. He looked un-strong, as if he might struggle to hold on. Unlike my Action Man, who not only had gripping hands but also realistic hair.

When driving, my dad rested the flat hands on the crossbar of the two-spoke steering wheel of his Austin Princess, a tinny piece of British engineering regression that was built (as if to symbolise national decline) by the next generation after the Spitfire and bouncing-bomb makers. He steered by calmly pushing this way and that on the wheel. He named all the cars we ever had Mo, short for motor, I suppose. 'Come on, Mo', when accelerating. 'A nice run for Mo', when belting down any straight road at an alarming rate. If we ever passed that white disc with a black line across, which *The Highway Code* tells you means the National Speed Limit applies, it was spotted with the cry: 'Fast as you like!' Not so much a cry, it was more a mimic of a yell, at spoken-voice level. He could never really be noisy; he was always constrained, unless he was whistling along to Max Bygraves songs in the kitchen, when he forgot himself. Despite his evident attachment to each car, Mo was always gone after two years to be replaced by a new Mo, in an effort to fend off the costs of depreciation. All costs pained him. It was in observing this bonding and casting aside that I could have learned not to trust my father's expressions of affection. I missed that indicator, though.

On a family outing, whether it was a short run to Epping or all the way to Venice via the Brenner Pass, I was always in the front passenger seat alongside him, perched up on a square of foam rubber, so the seatbelt wouldn't run across my neck. The foam had been covered neatly by my mother using spare fabric she had stitched together. She could have stitched her children together too, perhaps, in another life. My older brother and younger sister were in the back because they could co-exist peacefully whereas I could not, with either of them.

Sometimes I had to hold an Ordnance Survey map and I learned to identify churches, bridges, hospitals and railway lines. I was assigned to write in Dad's red notebook when he bought petrol. The number of gallons and the mileage:

'4 at—'

Then when the petrol gauge reached the halfway point:

'½ at—'

He showed me how to work out the car's fuel consumption in miles per gallon and I was delegated to write that in as well, '33', perhaps, or '34½'. I forget now how he made that calculation.

On a longer journey he'd have a homemade clipboard (with a bulldog clip at the top and a stubby pencil tied on with string) and he'd appoint me to write the time and distance covered at various points. The first always seemed to be:

'Chingford – 3.'

Chingford was consistently three miles from our house. We didn't move and neither did it. But I dutifully noted its existence every time we passed through on the way to the North Circular. He preferred me to quietly scribble down already known information, rather than perhaps be in charge of finding some good music on the radio. Not that he was ever going to shout, 'Turn it up!' when 'Brown Sugar' came on.

On one holiday drive up a mountain road, steering round his favoured hairpin bends, he asked something I didn't properly hear so I said:

'Pardon?'

Since I was twelve and not yet sullen.

He let out an exasperated breath as he glanced down to see which gear the car was in, and then repeated the question:

'Am I in *two*?'

'Yes,' I said, falling into the trap of issuing redundant information.

'That wasn't very good rally navigating.'

That parental cosh was always close at hand.

'Ask me again,' I pleaded, giving him the chance to

follow up with a scoffing noise. I'd failed a task and cruelly spoiled his enjoyment of the hairpin. He had never asked what gear he was in before and he never did again.

He'd been an amateur Car Club navigator in the fifties and early sixties, often taking part in all-night rally events on deserted public roads. If we were going down a country lane, he'd say: 'This is a good rally road,' and I'd imagine him hurtling along in the passenger seat of a souped-up Ford Anglia or Mini Cooper, flat-handedly folding OS maps in the dark with a tiny torch between his teeth. His trophies from those days rested only briefly in the flat hands before being exhibited in a glass cabinet at home, where they have remained for over fifty years.

He switched off his little torch, presumably at my mother's request (instruction?), when she had babies. It seemed he could never muster the enthusiasm for his children that he once had for the rallying that had been terminated by their arrival. That he might be killed, and Mum left on her own with us, was her concern, though there could have been an upside to that outcome, provided she didn't then go on to contract leukaemia. Instead, we were left with him and his surges of flat-handed rage.

When he hit me, he'd do it with the palm and the fingers. At the time, the unwritten rule was that parents could hit, but not with a clenched fist and only in a target area below the belt, around the legs. It wasn't the mild pain of the smack that was memorable, though, it was the grimacing ferocity on his face, the tightened-up sadness. The speed of his approach was his tell. He tried to make it noiseless but you knew when he was coming up the stairs three at a time instead of two, like a dog that has stopped barking and is readying to bite. He wasn't really like a dog, though; he was not playful, not loyal and not brave. He just had a free hand; the witness for the defence had died from blood cancer.

Whether he was advancing up the stairs or up the garden I was stilled by fear, tears brimming my eyes at the first swing and spilling down my cheeks before a follow-up harder palm came along, which it did if the sound of the first strike hadn't sated him.

He never apologised for anything, he'd just stride away and not mention it again. He slapped happiness out of me, like dust out of a carpet.

My siblings didn't comfort me. They only had one parent too and the wrong side of him was a bleak place to be. They were habitually allied to him and apparently complicit in a view of our family life that judged it would all be better without me. I never saw him hit either of them, his acolytes, his cowed minions.

I didn't believe Mum could see what was happening, despite being told by my shrinking set of grandparents that she was in heaven, with the vague implication that she was looking down. No one really seemed to believe this. It was unimaginable that her hand would descend from above to turn the flat-hand away, putting the fear of Mum in him.

The grandparents were diminishing both individually and collectively. They grew increasingly frail and began to expire one by one soon after Mum died.

But those flat hands. What prompts me to recall them now are wooden table tops. If I'm sitting at a wooden table that hasn't been polished to a shine, so it has a dry surface, with no oil in it, an absence of moisture, the kind of table that is almost papery to the touch, so you could easily brush crumbs from it, the texture of that unpolished wood, to me, is that of my father's hands. Arid and sapless, neither hot nor cold, with no clammy dampness or residue, I can imagine him not leaving a fingerprint, even on a cold glass, nothing left behind, no trace that he was ever there. And without the evidence, the mark, the tangible proof, how can you show where he's been? No prints, no witnesses, case dismissed.

For a while I shared a bedroom with my brother, who couldn't keep his hands off my toys, especially my teddy, which he would rough up in vigorous games played alone under his bedclothes. I'd ask him to return my teddy to me, but I'd have to wait for it to come back, battered, worn and smelling repellently of him. He'd crumple up my comics too, saying, 'You can still read them', but I wanted them in mint condition for ever. I was always unhappy when we were in that room together. I would often go to sleep in my dad's bed after Mum died, preferring to be put into my own bed only when my brother was asleep. I'd wake up the next morning not remembering the journey.

When our bickering became too much for my father to tolerate, my brother decamped to the box room at the top of the stairs, so I now had the back bedroom to myself. I still struggled to sleep, in the dark with the morning so far away, and continued on occasion to begin the night in Dad's room.

Sometimes I would fall out of bed and he would hear the impact from his seat in front of the television downstairs. He was usually sympathetic to the fallen, and the flat hands were ideal for tucking in sheets; he'd slide them between the mattress and the bed to cocoon me in a cotton–nylon mix. One night I fell out repeatedly, trying to land on a particular loose floorboard that made a good sound, in the hope that he would come up to reinstate me in the bed with a show of kindness. Instead, every bump overhead was driving him mad and when he eventually arrived he was furious.

'What *are* you *doing*?'

'I fell out.'

'Twenty times?'

'Not twenty . . .'

'For goodness' sake.'

He pushed the sheets under the mattress with such flat-handed force that I couldn't roll on to my side, and he went back downstairs knowing I wouldn't dare do it again. Still, that interaction was better than nothing, though I knew that the falling-out-of-bed option was now exhausted.

One day my flat-handed father wandered unannounced into my bedroom. The door never had a lock on it and there was no convention of knocking. It was broad daylight. Where was everyone? Why were we alone in the house? My sister may have been over the road visiting her friends, whose mother had become a surrogate for her. My brother? Who knows? My mother was dead.

My dad pushed the door to behind him, with his flat straight hand. There was a big window in my bedroom that looked out over the back garden. I had my back to this window, and there was a second, narrower, window to my left, which overlooked the sideway between our house and next door. In front of me were two single beds, mine was on my right nearest the doorway, which cut the corner of the room, and a spare bed was against the wall on my left. It was a bright room with astronaut wallpaper on one wall and footballers on the others.

My father was wearing only his white Y-fronts with their elasticated waistband. He was often in his underpants, there was nothing too unusual in that; he'd also mow the lawn in small blue swimming trunks. He seemed to like being partially dressed. He spent no money on clothes, wearing the same ones for years, or none at all.

I may have been getting changed when he came in. Maybe it was opportunistic on his part, maybe it wasn't premeditated, maybe he surprised himself.

That we came to be lying on one of the beds together with me naked and him in his Y-fronts was not my idea. The flat hands became very busy as his cuddling developed into caressing, all without speaking. It was a quiet, librarial molestation. I was largely motionless, he writhed and rubbed for a long time, it seemed like about two thousand hours.

He ran his hands over my back and my bottom; his face, with some stubble on it, was close to mine (maybe it was the afternoon, since he shaved every morning with an electric razor). I didn't like the feeling of the stubble. He didn't speak. He didn't kiss me. It was a bit unpleasant, but tolerable, given how nice it was to be cuddled. If your mother dies when you are six there is a significant drop-off in physical affection, a catastrophic collapse, an exponential retraction, followed by a flatline.

'This is our special cuddle. You must never tell anyone about this cuddle,' he said.

That self-serving parody of tenderness was an improvement on the norm so I went along with that plan. Then he left and I dressed. I wasn't shocked or emotional, neither tearful nor wanting to flee. I was just a bit confused, part grateful, part burdened by a new secret.

Did he put some clothes on and go about his business without a backward glance? Or did he contemplate burying me in Epping Forest before I could tell anyone? He was safe anyway, in that respect, because no one would ever believe what *I* said.

This was two or three years after Mum died. I was about eight or nine. He was in his early forties. He didn't come into my room, with that intent, for a further two or three years, which made that first instance a stand-alone occurrence, or a stand-alone opportunity perhaps.

Despite being prone to boasting and to bragging, and being frequently accused of Showing Off, I resisted flaunting my special-cuddle status to my siblings. I didn't ask them if he went into their rooms at night. I assumed he never cornered either of them alone. Had I let slip what was going on, I could then have jealously guarded the mystery of my unique family time with Dad, should they have started asking questions. Somehow I knew not to say a word, to collude. I can be trusted with a confidence to this day. I never tell.

I could keep this secret because I lacked the power to force news of it out of my person. Words to describe it adequately, or plausibly, were beyond me. I didn't want to tell anyway, not because I was consciously frightened, or even concerned that I'd be disbelieved, more that this new secrecy had gone very deep inside me, taken root so far within my being that to eject it was to risk self-destruction by somehow turning myself inside out and never being able to go back to where I was before. It felt, still feels, like a risk.

Maybe I wanted it to happen again, as it was affection of sorts. For his part, he must have known he could forge a constricting pact around me. Or was he, unconsciously, trying to sabotage the whole domestic set-up? Reaching out for the blessed relief of his children being taken away when the truth came out? In the absence of that thought (which has just occurred to me) he appeared to love me, in those intimate moments, more than he did his other two children, though all the evidence of our family life told otherwise.

For a couple of years there was a period of partition in the big back bedroom, which put the brakes on his ardour. We had a variety of housekeepers living in the box room who would cook, clean and look after us when we got home from school. So my brother had to come back into the twin room, and our conflict resumed.

One night I wound up my alarm clock, which had a very loud *tick-tock*, just to wind him up in turn. Soon after that our bedroom was divided by a thin wall into two tiny rooms. Dad could not now sneak into my room to coax me out from beneath the covers, or urge me to take off my pyjamas, since my brother was an unwitting sentry on the other side of the partition.

After two or three years the housekeeper experiment was abandoned and my brother skulked back to the box room, the divide came down and I was available again. I would venture far down under the covers to the bottom of my bed, where in the past I'd been afraid to go for fear of what might lurk there beneath my sheet, two blankets, eiderdown and an orange bedspread (it occurs to me now that the blue of the carpet and the orange of the bedspread reappeared when I decorated my kitchen twenty years later).

I kept toys with me under the covers, on all four sides of the bed, for protection. I was tucked in safely. Teddy was at the top, with me, then I had a blue plastic mouse's head from the top of a bubble-bath bottle, a small yellow and white rabbit and a pyjama case made by Granny Price, my mum's mum, that was modelled on Dougal from *The Magic Roundabout*. The four of them guarded me in the bed, until the door opened and I would be brought up from under the covers and invited to take off my pyjamas by a man in his underpants. After that I had to lie or kneel naked on the bed and be fondled by those cadaverous hands, those bloodless mannequin's replicas, with the Y-fronts visible in the gloom. The library silence continued as he concentrated on his work before he would abruptly rush out. I never knew where he went, or why so suddenly.

I'm sure I could still discern my father's touch today. If I lay naked in a darkened room and people I have known roamed, flat-handed, over my back and behind, I doubt I could identify any of them other than my father. Maybe I'd be jolted into recollection if my mother's hands reached out through time and across dimensions, but that particular dry stroke, like someone testing wood for knots, would, I'm sure, be instantly recognisable to me. I bet I'd jump six feet in the air.

Eventually I began to resist audibly and he stopped, presumably for fear of my siblings hearing. The last time he did it I was thirteen and I became erect, which is still unbearably embarrassing. Did he sense it? I tried to keep it away from him but I was unable to contort myself indefinitely; we were lying next to each other and I was partly on my side and partly on my back. I remember clearly deciding to allow my nubile cock to sink into the flesh of his tummy. He did not flinch or acknowledge what was happening. He made no attempt to flat hand it away, to juggle it about, like half a hot dog sausage between two table tennis bats. After a minute or two of noticeably shallower breathing on his part, he bolted from the room. Normally afterwards he would return to his bed and I'd put my pyjamas back on and try to sleep, so it was a shock a few minutes later when he came back in. He leant in to me in the dark, as I lay under the covers, and said:

'If any white stuff comes out, don't worry about it, it's perfectly normal.'

I didn't respond. Did he imagine he was teaching me about erections and ejaculation, as if this was a kind of sex education lesson? I avoided his gaze in the dark, lying still, mentally rolling my eyes and waiting for him to leave. What did he think I was, a child?

Ashes

My dad came into the room and shut the door behind him. He looked serious. It was my bedroom. He told me to sit on the bed. He sat down next to me. This was unusual. He was right up close to me. I didn't feel like I was in trouble. Then he put his arm around me, which was even more unusual. I wondered what he was going to do. I was six, nearly six and a half. What did he want with me?

'Now, be brave,' he said. 'Mummy's gone to heaven.'

Other than my mum, I've never known of a person who was terminally ill not being told that they were. That's not to say that it's never happened but no one has said to me that a similar thing occurred with a relative of theirs, no one has said that they once read about a case like that, or that there are passages on the subject in novels by Dostoyevsky and Dickens and Victor Hugo and Vikram Seth and Chimamanda Ngozi Adichie, since it is such a widespread practice around the world.

There aren't, and it isn't.

I've never heard of an instance in life, fiction, rumour, gossip or hearsay, of a sick woman not being informed that she was dying as the expressed wish of her own husband.

Never mind that her children and sister should not be told either.

When people learn that my mother was kept unaware she was terminally ill they frequently settle on the comforting notion that it was a different time, and that: 'It wouldn't happen now.'

It's commonplace to believe that the present day, right now as you read this, represents the sharp end of human progress, which can be measured not just in advances in medical science, long-haul journey times and download speed, but also by honesty in palliative care. There is a reassuring belief that human behaviour is on an improvement continuum.

By its own logic this tells us that what happened to Mum was the norm in the seventies. Terminally ill patients must have been gathered together in wards, in mutual ignorance of their own impending departures, with all their friends and relatives collectively in on the deception. This imaginary scenario falls apart when previous visitors to the bedsides of the dying become incurably sick themselves, and arrive on the ward where they once kept secrets from a now lost relative. As a method of palliative care it's unsustainable.

It's more likely that it was unusual for someone not to be told they are dying, that normally the first person to know would be the patient. 'How long have I got, Doc? Give it to me straight,' seems more plausible than, 'How long has she got, Doctor? And let's not upset her by telling her.'

If the quality of palliative care is improving then a journey back through history ought to reveal an increasing lack of concern for the dying and the dead, until we arrive at a period where barely a thought is given to a funeral or any act of remembrance. Yet the one thing that appears to connect all ancient civilisations, regardless of geography or time, is the importance of their tombs, mausoleums and burial grounds.

In my family, when Mum was dying, the stated policy was:

'Least said, soonest mended.'

Not a motto you'll see framed on the wall of any funeral parlours.

Yet these were the words of tiny, stooped Granny Davies to Granny Price in relation to the death of her eldest daughter. Dad agreed that it would be better for the children not to know Mummy was dying, and therefore they should not be part of the end game, the mourning, or any subsequent recollection of her life.

So when Mum died pictures of her were taken down, there were no photo albums, no clothes, virtually nothing for me to remember her by at all, just a few books and her green Wedgwood trinket boxes and her silver hairbrush and her red address book by the phone and these memories:

—Her collecting me from infants' school, after an accident in Mrs Gomer's class during story time. I'd raised myself up on my haunches and a puddle had formed on the polished wood floor, which I showed to the boy next to me. Mrs Gomer sent me to the headmistress, Miss Philips, who had a chest of drawers full of children's clothes. I chose some navy blue shorts and then I was out by the school gates with Mum, no one else was about, and she said:

'What are those shorts?'

And I said:

'They're my PE shorts.'

And she said:

'You haven't got any PE shorts.'

And we went home early, which was a treat.

—My brother had been hogging our toy spud gun and not letting me have a go, and I was frustrated, and when Mum picked me up, from those same gates, she handed me a small, white paper bag and inside was a brand-new, identical metal spud gun, with none of the black paint chipped off it by my brother. How did she know I wanted one? No one has ever given me a gift since that could match that. I've told people to stop trying, as it's not possible.

—There was a man at our house doing some painting and I saw him outside the back door and he was drinking a cup of tea and chatting to Mum and I asked him what his name was and he said: 'Engelbert Humperdinck,' and Mum laughed and I didn't understand why, so I asked again, since what he'd said didn't sound like a real name, and he said: 'Engelbert Humperdinck' again and she laughed again, and it was clear I wasn't going to get anywhere with this, so I just hung around.

—I went to have my troublesome tonsils and adenoids out. Dad tried to cheer me up by saying Dr Grunberger had said he was going to 'throw them in the dustbin'. But a nurse woke me at six in the morning the next day and made me eat cornflakes, which felt like swallowing tiny ninja throwing stars, and I hadn't slept well because the boy and girl either side of me whispered all night and got out of their beds, and when it was time to go I couldn't lift my bag in the corridor and I was only five and I was tearful, and then Mum said my name and I looked up and she smiled and picked up my bag and held my hand and it was so nice to see her.

—I had put a wooden block into a toothpaste box and made a rattle out of it but I'd lost it and Mum realised it had gone in the dustbin and then a bin man was at the front door with my homemade toy and he seemed to understand how special it was and she let me think he was wonderful and didn't tell me she'd asked him to look out for it, as she must have done.

—I would lie on my back on the carpet with my feet in the air and move my legs apart, and then together again, back and forth, like windscreen wipers, and Mum would laugh and ask me to show her friends, which I did, and they always laughed too.

—We walked quickly to nursery in Loughton one day and I grazed my knee on the way even though I was holding Mum's hand, and I cried when she left me, but then I was distracted by a kind lady and did some colouring with crayons on a chain of paper men. It was nicer than the playgroup in Chingford where I'd been afraid of the bigger children. She didn't take me there again. Although that may be because we moved house when I was two. I still have the paper men.

And those are my memories, along with a few others dotted through these pages, of six years with Mum. I don't remember the sound of her voice.

*

Sixteen years later, Granny Price told me about the decision made at the hospital. We were sitting in her annexe on
the side of her younger daughter Hazel's single-storey home
in Adelaide, behind the screen door out of the heat. As she
talked she tipped the dregs of a cup-a-soup on to a saucer,
as lunch for her ancient cat Fritz, who, judging by the size
of him, might have been supplementing his diet elsewhere.

Gran said there had been two doctors who disagreed over
it, but the idea held sway that Mum would be too upset,
with three young children, to cope with her prognosis.
Granny said one doctor had wanted to tell Mum and the
other one didn't, and that she herself had wanted to tell
Mum but my dad and Granny Davies said not to, and she
was quietened. Granny didn't even write to Australia to tell
Hazel, so that Mum would be certain to pass to the other
side in ignorance.

And she seemed sure that Mum never knew right to the
end, but there was so much pain in the recollection and she
blinked away her sadness and we moved to another subject.

My Australian cousins have told me that when the letter
came from England to say that Auntie Shirley had died,
their mum sat on the back porch and cried for three days.
And years later when my eldest cousin was due to go over-
seas and visit England he asked Gran if she'd like him to
break Uncle Roy's legs for her. She said no, so he didn't
bother visiting my dad.

The decision not to tell her feels hostile to Mum. Her
chance to try to manage her children's feelings was taken
away, and she was faced with half-truths and untruths in
her final days. It seems misogynistic; would a man not be
told he was dying because he had three small children and
he'd be upset?

But would she not have thought she was dying? Was she so weak that she was unable to push for an answer? Was she barely eating, sleeping most of the day, under sedation and full of deadening morphine? Her immune system unable to defend her, her skin white, bruises appearing at the slightest touch, nosebleeds, a painful swollen spleen? Could she manage to look at her own charts? Or suspect that she was not getting better? Did she notice that the times when she felt well enough to go home were becoming more infrequent, and shortening in duration? Could she not ask them to tell her the truth? Could she speak?

Perhaps she knew all along. Perhaps she colluded with the charade. She looked at her husband and saw someone unable to discuss his feelings, or her feelings, or to empathise with his children, and she knew that he might fall apart, that he needed to move through this in silent denial, almost wishing it to be over. Perhaps she worried about how he felt as she lay dying, perhaps he looked tired and drawn and frightened and she was more concerned about him. Perhaps he said:

'What am I going to do?'

Then her impending death was seen to be a problem for him, that she could only help to solve by going quietly, certainly not by involving her sister, who might fly in from Adelaide with all kinds of notions about what was best, and also by not telling the children, who would have questions he couldn't answer and shed tears he wouldn't want to see. Perhaps she felt awful for what she was doing to him by being terminally ill. So she saw fewer and fewer people as she became more and more tired, just her husband and her parents by the end.

Dad needed to control the nightmare he was living

through, to hush those around him who might have been at odds with his view, and this later became an area of practised expertise for him. We were all duly silenced.

Least said, soonest mended.

Hospitals are not new. They go back about two and a half thousand years, often established by the prevailing religion of a place. Many of these institutions still bear the names of saints, like St Margaret's where Mum died. Universal free health care was only established in Britain in the form of the National Health Service in 1948, with the unforeseen consequence that now anyone could pass a dying relative over to a state-funded institution. In some parts of the world, the family home has to accommodate the terminally ill, as was once the case in all countries. In the past, before the NHS at least, it would be difficult to avoid seeing dead people, usually your own relations, but now no one has to see a corpse, never mind tend to someone as they rot from the inside out. Despite a history of quarantine for the carriers of known contagions, only recently has the desire to pass on the ailing and afflicted become an achievable reality for all. Now the sick can die with their own thoughts, rather than their own family.

This began with improvements in diagnosis (leukaemia was named by a German physician, Rudolf Virchow, who was among those making advances in pathology in the mid-nineteenth century). Knowing how a person is going to die, and exactly what is happening to them while they do, is something to which families have only recently had to adapt. That knowledge can seem an unnecessary burden for the patient, presumably that's what they thought when they were discussing Mum. That it was best not to let her know for *her* sake.

If you were dying, would you want to know?

I would. I'd then prefer to donate all usable organs, before being dismembered for medical science, with what's left minced, sautéed and served to zoo animals in a tin bowl.

Ask yourself the question and share your answer, at the first symptom of something bad, because you may end up in the hands of people who decide for you. It's difficult to consider it when you're healthy as the mind provides little space for death planning. My own thoughts turn flippantly to the horror of checking out during the football season without seeing the final table. I hope my close of play comes during the cricket season, though not halfway through a Test Match, of course. Perhaps imminent oblivion might cure me of the sports fixation that has often provided a distraction from harsh realities.

Nowadays, with people living longer and an increase in dementia sufferers, caring for loved ones at home is common again. For cancer patients the painful decline is often best managed in a hospice but dying at home is an option preferred by many. Once that choice has been made the herbalists and homeopaths begin to circle, juice diets and prayer are deployed, before death arrives, possibly followed by a psychic or two offering to contact the deceased for a fraudulent consideration.

Dying among your close family, with their care being your last human contact, is not a twenty-first-century development born of more progressive times, but a return to the norm of human existence.

What happened to my mum was not normal.

What if you were dying and you didn't know? But everyone else knew. They had colluded not to tell you. Your three children are kept away. There is no telephone. You're in a room not knowing you are dying and you're just wondering why all the treatments aren't working. You don't feel any better, you feel worse. Eventually you're barely able to drag your withering frame out of bed and to the toilet. Perhaps you wonder if you're dying. You miss your children so much every minute of every day. They are all you can think about. No one appears to understand this.

Your husband comes to see you. He knows you are dying. Then he goes away again. Your father comes to see you. He knows you are dying. He goes away again. Two doctors come to see you, they know you are dying, one of them is of the view that you shouldn't know you are dying, the other keeps quiet. They don't tell you because you're a mother of three and, as a woman, emotional. Palliative care is easier if the patient can be guided into the dark without any awkward displays of hysterical grief. They think it best you don't know. You might not be able to cope. They decide to keep you there and deceive you until your body gives out. Just die, please, without anyone having to see anyone crying. No one wants that.

Your husband's mother knows you are dying and she feels that not only should you not know that you are dying but your children shouldn't either. They are never told you are going to be leaving them for ever. They are in a house a little over six miles away. They are brought to see you in hospital, but not often. When you die no one will talk to them about you. Your picture will be taken down. They will be told you are in heaven and to be brave. They will have no keepsake from you.

With all the lies and deceit already in place how can your death be anything but a relief? For days now they have been waiting for you to die but instead you keep writing little letters to your husband, which he will never read to his children.

Luckily your only sibling lives in South Australia. Out of sight, out of mind. If she was here she'd want to see you all the time, she'd possibly be of the opinion that you have the right to know what is happening to you. What a mess she would create; it's better for everyone if she is kept out of this. So you never say goodbye to her either. She never says goodbye to you. You never have a conversation about all the times you spent together. She doesn't come to see you.

Instead, you are confronted every visiting time by the peculiar twitching eyes of those who know you are dying but prefer to keep that to themselves. Leaving you with no chance to organise some aftermath, write journals, letters, little notes, to preserve and express the love you feel in a way that will nourish those you leave behind, so that at the very least they know it was not their fault. No letter. No goodbye. You fall asleep and never wake up. You die.

Everyone is relieved that they don't have to keep up the performance any longer. Thank goodness for that. It was so difficult for them, pretending to you that you were going to go home. It was so difficult for them to tell the children, who were eight, six and three, that they couldn't 'go to see Mummy today', when they really meant: 'ever see Mummy again'.

You are dead but the secrets can continue. As if it is the secrets that sustain these fucking people.

The new secret is that your little girl mustn't be told that you have died. So her brothers are told not to tell her. 'Don't tell your sister that Mummy has gone to heaven.' Yes, that means your little six-year-old boy who has lost his mummy will share this secret with the grown-ups. He has crossed some age threshold, old enough both to know you are dead and to learn that death is secret. The thing he will remember about you dying is his three-year-old sister asking when they can go to visit you and the pleasant feeling of the power he'd been granted in being able to say:

'Not today.'

'When *can* we go?' she said.

'Maybe tomorrow.'

And she asked again and again.

Of course they all had power over you. They preferred to keep you there in ignorance; they had all the cards, your husband and his little mother. They had you penned in, they had control; the children won't know, the sister won't know, you won't know. You are powerless, you are silenced, you are theirs. And your husband will look sad and you, in your final days, will try to lift him with encouraging and supportive words, and you will be hoping to go home as soon as you can, because it must be difficult for him, coping without you. You feel terrible that you are ill, just look at him, it's so hard for him. 'I'm sorry,' you say.

Phew. Finally you died. That went on for ages.

NO MOURNING. Your children will go away for a few days when the funeral is happening. You will be burned and the forgetting will begin. They will be told separately of their mother's death. They will never see each other's grief, which will be limited to a few minutes individually with your husband. They won't be told where you are laid to rest. They won't know where to go to speak to you, to ask you anything, to remember you.

But you will never be forgotten. Because the middle one, the six-year-old, will write about you, he'll say that he remembers your kindness and your warmth and how much you laughed together when you put him in the bath while he still had his socks on.

For years I wondered where Mum's grave was. I had an idea, possibly from something said, that it was in Harlow, Essex. I had a friend, when I was sixteen, who lived there and he said there was a crematorium and cemetery at the end of his road, past the famous footballer Glenn Hoddle's house. We went up there and he helped me to look for her, and I should have thanked him for that kindness. We buzzed in on noisy 50cc motorbikes, turned off the engines, and were immediately quietened by the absolute silence of the place. There were scores of white headstones on lawns sloping down away from the car park. With barely a word, we split up and searched for her. There was no sign of a grave with her name on it and I was beginning to think we were in the wrong place. We walked up to the single-storey modern crematorium and were greeted by a caretaker who told us that everything was closed as it was a Sunday. I told him I thought my mum was there and he fetched some keys and unlocked a small hexagonal building that contained the leather-bound book of remembrance. He asked me if I knew the date of her death so I told him and he turned the large, nearly square pages to the one for August 22nd and there was her name, Shirley Margaret Davies, in elegant calligraphy. We told him she wasn't in the graveyard and he directed us to where urns containing ashes were buried, an area of woodland divided into the twelve months. In the section for August there were some plaques, flower holders or photographs, but there was nothing for Mum. We left, and as the years go by sometimes I remember

August 22nd and sometimes I don't. I went there in 1992, on the twentieth anniversary, with my then girlfriend, who had a shaved head with a grown-out Mohican on top that tumbled down the back of her leather jacket, and ripped jeans patched underneath with floral fabrics. She was older than me, only five years younger than Mum when she died, and she consoled me tenderly as I sobbed, as I'd never done on any anniversary before, kneeling on the earth dropping tears among the buried urns. She stroked my back and I asked her to stop and she sat with me in silence, for which kindness I should have thanked her.

I asked my father about the lack of a plaque for Mum when his brother, my Uncle Pat, died and was taken to the same crematorium in 2011. We were standing only yards from her hidden resting place. He told me he'd wanted to scatter Mum's ashes in Epping Forest since she'd loved it so much, but the crematorium had buried the urn and there was no record of the exact spot. Once again it was as if this had happened to him, not that he had neglected to provide any kind of memorial for his children's mother. It was unclear how long the crematorium had held the ashes for collection before they decided to bury them in an unmarked spot.

It was the first conversation we'd had about her dying since he came in to my bedroom in 1972, and sat down with me on the end of my bed, and put his arm around me and looked serious and told me to be brave, and said that Mummy had gone to heaven, and I began to cry because I loved her so much and she was my friend, and he said 'be brave', and I cried and he said 'be brave' and I knew to stop crying, and he said 'be brave', and I knew that crying was not the thing to do, since he was not crying and I had seen no one crying over Mummy's death. She was in heaven now and there wouldn't be any further conversations, and he didn't mention my brother and then he told me not to tell my sister and then he went out and shut the door behind him and I had stopped crying and I was on my own. I felt that loneliness for many years, really, until I had children of my own.

Gardens

I was at the top of the garden, sulking, moping about and waving a bamboo cane around. Everyone else was indoors. I must have done something that led to my being alone up there, outside when everyone else went inside. Perhaps some flash of contrariness or intransigence that ruined a game and led to a closing of ranks around our dad.

Mum used to grow tomatoes and runner beans in the greenhouse at the far end of the garden, next to the rhubarb patch and the blackberry brambles on the back fence, and she used bamboo to support her plants, which explains how I came to be swinging a cane around one afternoon a few years after she died, swishing it vigorously through the air so it made a sound. I whacked it hard against the badminton net post, hoping to be seen from the house, petulantly demonstrating how upset and isolated I felt.

I was doing it partly for attention and partly because it's enjoyable to hit things with sticks. When my Auntie Hazel had Alzheimer's she memorably said, as she walked slowly along aided by her daughter: 'I wish I had a stick,' followed after a pause with, 'and someone to hit.'

The top half of my bamboo cane broke off, spun thirty feet up the garden and decapitated one of Mum's roses beyond the goal net. Pale yellow petals burst out and fell to the ground. I looked down the garden to the big kitchen window, which offered an uninterrupted view, its wisteria border pruned around the edge of the frame. Dad was there and he'd seen me. He was already on the move.

In later years when a football went through a window into the greenhouse it would disturb only weeds. The broken glass would join other similar shards and Dad would express his lack of surprise that his sons were so inept with their Brazilian banana kicks. He spiced his exasperation with a detectable measure of sadness over this besmirching of Mum's memory, so his offspring would know they'd caused him pain. This offspring noticed that, anyway. It felt opportunistic on his part, since none of the panes were ever repaired.

Behind the goal net was a wall about three feet high, so that the garden sloped from the back fence and then became a bed of around a dozen mature rose bushes, before it dropped vertically at the wall, becoming flat for fifty feet or so. The rest of the lawn sloped down to the patio. The rose prickles punctured many plastic footballs, but their blooms in all their various colours were to remain as a memorial to Mum.

It was therefore best not to be seen hacking any of them to pieces.

The flat area became a football pitch and after turning to mud in the winter it was turfed in the summer and carefully whitewashed into a badminton court by my dad. He'd pop the caps off two holes in the ground and insert green metal net posts, the standard 5 feet 1 inch tall (the net *must* be five feet high in the centre). I swung on one of those once and snapped it. My dad took me with him to the local Back

Garden Sporting Supplies Emporium, where, to my relief, it was ingeniously repaired by the insertion of a broom handle to connect the two halves of tube.

The whitewashing was done with a little truck that was pushed along, with a wide wheel in the middle laying down the lines. Wooden posts, bashed in with a wooden mallet and with string tied around, gave a guideline to follow. A badminton court is forty-four feet long and twenty feet wide and the flattened part of our garden could just contain it. It's hard to believe the dimensions were anything but exact.

The marking of borders, which he would then police keenly during play, was important to Dad. Games had rules and boundaries and lines. Sports clubs had fixtures in which there was accurate scoring and an indisputable outcome and time spent in such a game could be seen as socialising and all of it served as an opportunity to be a decent chap by playing fair and shaking hands afterwards. The etiquette was everything: don't return serve if the ball lands out, take a bit of pace off when serving to a lady, don't dispute the opponent's line call. On and on went the myriad rules, written and unwritten: pay your subs, don't park in the Captain's space, the ladies make the cakes.

All of it now seems at odds with Dad's latent reservoir of desire, which was not cold and still, but hot, and threatening to bubble over. Of course all that order appealed to him, those lines and rules and agreed limits and outcomes, an imposed structure of acceptable behaviour at a club where you had to be the right sort of fellow to become a member in the first place. In accountancy, too, his profession, the numbers, the columns, adding up correctly not incorrectly, with restrictions imposed from the outside in the form of rules and laws. Order, order and more order, all complied with, all helping to conceal what lies within him, but at what cost? Where could the pressure be released? Perhaps at home, where there were no outsiders to determine boundaries. But even there he marked out some of his own in whitewash.

Unfortunately, it was difficult to control the direction of a shuttlecock in the breeze at the top of the garden, and to be strict about service boxes and tramlines when playing in the wind with children was hopeless, so eventually our not being able to do it right meant we ended up not doing it at all.

Each summer I watched Dad mark those lines. I might be allowed a little go on the whitewash truck but my memory is of a man keen to mark out the perfect court, not someone who'd give his unreliable son the chance to paint a line that looked like a failed lie-detector test. He made it look difficult and part of me felt that he needed relieving of his duty. Maybe I'd have rushed the job, gone a bit wrong here and there in trying to take pleasure from the experience, but really, who gives a fuck?

Everything had to be done properly. We once played pitch and putt on holiday. There were nine holes. At the first tee, I took a swipe at the ball (we'd never done this before) and knocked it about two inches. My sister thought this hilarious, and laughed even more when I did it again. So I did it again and again, and now she was really laughing, I was laughing too, and eventually on the eighth try I belted the thing in the direction of the hole. Dad had not been laughing, he was irritated, so the rest of the round was solemn, apart from when he managed a hole-in-one. At the end, he totted up the scores. I knew I'd beaten them all, but Dad included all of my silly swings at the first tee in my total, so I lost to my brother. Not that it bothered me, as you can tell.

On a hot day he'd mark out the badminton court wearing only his old blue swimming trunks and no deodorant. Sweat would drip like dew from his nose while his *Brilliantine* hair stayed in place and the sagging rear of his little bathers gathered high in the crack between his cheeks.

I'd usually be wearing a football shirt: an Arsenal one bought when I was five (number five sewn on the back by Mum) or a stylish red and black Manchester City away top. There is a photo from 1971 of my brother in the Arsenal shirt and me in the City one, grinning happily on a bench together, with him showing off a plastic football marked 'Arsenal Double Champs', which must have pained Dad as a Tottenham Hotspur fan. After Mum died I wisely continued to support Arsenal, and my brother followed Dad's beloved Spurs, which didn't help sibling relations.

I still have those little shirts. I treasure them, knowing that Mum saw me in them, watched me play, put them in the wash and handed them back clean, with the little badges and numbers sewn on by her hand.

After she died Dad never bought me another football shirt. His mantra was:

'Take your shirt *off*!'

This could come from anywhere in the garden, he wasn't always in sight, so it would sometimes make me start, this instruction to expose myself to the sun. Sometimes he'd open the kitchen window to yell it, and I'd sheepishly unveil my spindly torso, until he wasn't looking, then I'd put my shirt back on.

Dad used to comment on how unsightly it was for me

to have brown arms only up to my short sleeves, beneath which I was typically English (which in all other respects would be seen as a plus). He started to look for cap-sleeved T-shirts for me to wear so my arms would be a uniform brown and not so unattractive.

On beach holidays he'd apply a coin-sized dab of sun-cream to my shoulders. Every summer the skin would burn and peel off. He would claim that brown skin would appear underneath once the dead skin had peeled away, which was nonsense but it was widely believed, and no one had heard of cancerous melanomas. He applied calamine lotion to my sunburnt back, a job he took his time over.

Dad's own efforts to tan included rolling the top down on his trunks and smiling as his pubes popped out. 'Going brown' was a national obsession. People would say: 'What's the point of going on holiday if you don't go brown?'

Despite being a hopeless footballer, Dad always encouraged games on the beach and in the garden, particularly cricket. I struggled with batting since I hated getting out, often denying that a ball had hit the stumps behind me, or I'd be in trouble for smashing it as hard as I could, clearing the laurel bushes and nearly killing Mrs Newby next door. I once set off the Newbys' burglar alarm by hitting a window with a plastic boomerang that Auntie Hazel had sent from Australia. I had expected it to come back. Dad told us that Mr Newby had climbed the Matterhorn with his sons, a staggering achievement that he hoped to emulate. I felt a disappointment to him, since that plainly was not on the cards for our family, who couldn't get round a pitch and putt course without falling out. Perhaps he imagined scaling the peak with his two sons while his young daughter stayed at base camp with his wife. But she died so that was scuppered.

We played with a real cricket ball and protective batting gloves. My brother once told me to take them off because they were getting dirty, and then the ball trapped my thumb against the bat handle. A blood blister the size of my eye appeared, though I couldn't see it properly since my actual eyes were bucketing tears. Dad was forced to rebuke my brother, a rare and pleasing event that gave me an insight into how nice it must have felt for him, all those times I was told off.

When I was sent to secondary school a year early Dad was disappointed that I couldn't get into the cricket team. In my second year he told me to mention that I was still young enough to play with the first years. The master in charge looked perplexed but gave me a chance. My team-mates couldn't understand what I was doing there since I was in the year above. I remember arguing about fielding positions with an enormous idiot from East House who inexplicably thought he was a faster runner than me. To them my dropping down a year marked me out as a hopeless case. I had no desire to be in their year even though I didn't feel at home in mine.

'Did you get any runs?' said Dad.

'One,' I said.

Fail.

'One? Where did you bat?'

'Eleven,' I said.

Eleven is the last man in.

'Eleven!' he said.

Fail.

'Yes.'

'Did you get any wickets?'

'They wouldn't let me bowl.'

'Wouldn't let you bowl?'

'No.'

Fail.

'Why not?'

'They just didn't.'

He didn't ask if I'd enjoyed it. I knew he wanted to be proud of my sporting prowess, but that was my only game of any kind for the school. I never earned a special tie for sport.

At home most warm days were spent in the garden, playing cricket or on the swing, or climbing the ash tree. In the autumn we'd pick apples and wrap them in pages of the *Sunday Times Magazine* before storing them in the shed. In the winter my brother and I would take shots at each other in goal, in all weathers, until it went dark. We'd have to peel off our muddy jeans and leave them to soak in the bath, before eating Bovril on toast, tea cakes with jam, and slices of Battenberg (named after the German town of Battenberg from where a German Prince came to marry an English Princess leading to the creation of the name Mountbatten). We called it church window cake, as Dad had probably done when he was a boy, during the war, when the windows of his home in Chingford were blown in by a German bomb as the family sheltered under a table.

At teatime, somewhat disregarding our little sister, Dad would put on *Two Little Boys*, by the popular children's entertainer Rolf Harris, a song about sibling love by a now convicted sex offender. I'm not sure if there is irony at work here, or serendipity, or if it's just that circumstances have revealed the horrific double-hindsight that brotherly love is not inevitable, and that bad men will spend a lifetime constructing a charming façade.

The roses were all in bloom the day I whacked the badminton post with bamboo, as were all Mum's other flowerbeds and the rockery she'd built. Had she been in the garden, trowel in hand, kneeling on an old floor mat from a car, maybe she'd have seen that I hadn't meant to do it. At the time I thought it must have looked deliberate to Dad in the kitchen, as if I'd thrown the cane directly at the roses rather than hitting the post causing the end to break off. He strode towards me. I couldn't move. We used to say 'I was petrified' at school to mean really frightened. My eyes filled with tears, and there was no one on their knees nearby, looking up, peeling off a glove and saying:

'What's going on? He didn't mean to do it. It was an accident.'

She might have said that, and he might have said, as he sometimes did:

'There's no such thing as an accident.'

'If you hit him I will come for you with these secateurs and cut your rotting swimming trunks off before I set about your grim little todger, you sadistic bastard.'

She wouldn't have said that. It's just one of the violent fantasies I have largely left out of these pages. In one chapter now discarded, I metamorphosed into a mountain-lion-beast, and peeled my father's skin off in strips before pulping it with my conical fangs and sharp papillae. His remains then dissolved into the grass beneath my paws and disappeared for ever, while my siblings were nearby looking for him and not recognising me.

As he approached me in the garden I'm not going to say I split his skull with a giant claw. I'll just say what I remember so clearly. I knew he wasn't going to inspect the roses, gather the fallen petals and implore me to take more care, or tell me about each plant and which was Mum's favourite. I knew that he wasn't going to let me explain and that he wasn't going to yell at me, the neighbours might hear that. I knew he was going to hit me. I didn't run. I've always found crying and running difficult, however dramatic it looks in the cinema. My cheeks were awash. He was now standing over me. My cowering seemed to annoy him as it made me a difficult target. I was saying that it was an accident. He wore a look that said: 'Don't tell lies.' Gripping my arm with his left hand, he swung for my legs with his right. Three good contacts later he was back down the garden. He never mentioned it again. He didn't go to look at the roses. I was left crying. One of the lessons of my childhood I have yet to unlearn is that crying is something you do alone.

Lanterns

I walk out of the school gates and turn left. I'm not going with Luke today. I often walk home with him. He's in the same class as me at Staples Road. He's not very chatty but we live near each other so he's my best friend.

The other day Luke was carrying a Chelsea bag. It had a shoulder strap. We don't normally have bags at school, unless we are going swimming. I asked him why he supported Chelsea and he said he liked blue. Then I asked him what was in his bag and he opened it to show me a Police Range Rover. I asked him why he only had that in there and what was the point of the bag when he could just carry the car in his hand? He looked down and then he wasn't very chatty, as usual. He must like the bag and the Range Rover, though it seems annoying to have to carry a bag, and no one plays with toy cars at school anyway.

There is another boy who lives nearer to me but we're not really friends, even though he's only two doors down. We live in detached houses so two doors is quite far. There are driveways and steps up to our front doors. You don't often see people. This boy's dad has long hair, some of it is blond, some of it is fair, the rest is brown. He wears plimsolls. My dad isn't friendly with him, or anyone on our road.

No one comes to our house. When Mum was alive people sometimes came. There was one friend she had who had been to Ecuador and who gave me my stuffed frog. If you sit it in your palm you can't see the stitches, which go up its tummy. I think she worked for Shell (Mum's friend, not the frog).

The dyed-hair man two doors down has a Range Rover, a real one, it's massive; I had a lift in it once, you have to climb up on to the big leather seats but from inside you can see over all the other cars. The dad was chatty and so was the boy. I didn't say much but I really liked the car. One day my dad was driving along in our Austin and I said that the Spanish boy who lived next door had told me that the neighbour with the Range Rover had overtaken five cars at once on Loughton High Road. Dad sort of made a sound but without properly making one. It was an unsmiling noise. He did it quite often. Then I asked if we could get a Range Rover and he laughed:

'Ha ha HA HA!'

He still wasn't smiling, just making laughing sounds. It seemed like Dad couldn't stand Mr Next-Door-But-One, even though he lived on the same road, and was a dad, and had a good car. Normally Dad loves cars; he gets every issue of *Autocar* magazine.

The Spanish boy next door tells fibs. An RAF jet flew over the playground once and he said: 'That's my uncle,' and then he said he had another uncle who played for Barcelona, though that might have been because I had taken a Johan Cruyff card into school. It was a moving card, so if you tilted it he volleyed a ball.

As I walk along I stay close to the school fence and look down at my black Tuf school shoes, sticking out from beneath my itchy black school trousers. My grey school shirt is tucked in. I don't have to wear a tie. I don't have to wear any of these things, in fact, as the school doesn't have a uniform and most kids wear jeans and trainers, but Dad wanted me and my brother to wear uniforms, even though it actually makes us stand out instead of being the same as everyone else. My brother has left now and gone to secondary school. He didn't talk to me in the playground anyway.

It feels safer to have the fence close to me. My shoulder is brushing against it. I can see the waste-patch on the other side, which is the end of the playground where we are allowed to go when it's not raining. There are bushes and a fallen tree, some long grass and bits of stony clay. It's a great place to play war as there is a low wall down the middle, which is good for cover when you want to machine gun someone. It's also where you go to have a fight, as it's a bit further from the school than the rest of the playground. I once had to meet a fat kid there three playtimes in a row to fight him. He was in the year below but he was enormous. I didn't even know him but he wanted to fight me for some reason. It was horrible. In the end it was a draw, since neither of us was crying.

When the fence ends a row of houses begins. The front doors of these are close to the pavement; you can reach out and touch them without even stepping on to their little paths. On the other side of the road is Epping Forest.

I can feel loose chips of tarmac under my feet as I walk. It's nice to crunch them. I don't want to see Luke or anyone else. Coming up on the left is the steep alleyway that goes down to The Drive, which is quite a long street that comes out on Loughton High Road. Normally I would walk down there so I could go home past the shops but today I keep going. It makes me wonder if anyone has seen me take a different route. Is someone going to be suspicious? It's a hot day. The forest is bright green and there isn't much water in the brook at the bottom of Staples Road.

At the crossroads I could go straight over to go home along Nursery Road and past the big house called Dragons but I turn left into Forest Road, which will bring me out on to the High Road close to St Mary's, where the Cubs meet in the hall, and where we have our Church Parade every month, which Granny Price always comes to. I am not allowed to carry a flag on parade yet, as I'm not old enough. You have to wear a leather belt with a round flag holder that the pole sits in. I hate Cubs but I would like to have that job.

It's quiet on Forest Road. The houses here are small. There are two pubs near the top with the same car park. Before I reach the High Road I pass The Lantern Room Bistro. It's owned by the mum and dad of a boy in my class and is the only restaurant in Loughton, apart from the Wimpy and the Eastern Eye. I've never been in any of them.

When we put on *Alice in Wonderland* at school I thought I'd get a big part as I was top of the class but I had to play the cook and had no lines. I was told I could throw some pots and pans around, but there was only one pot and I had to pretend to stir it. It had SOUP written on it in big letters but I didn't have it facing the right way so you could only see that it was soup if you were at the side. Dad came to the performance.

'I thought you were going to throw pots and pans around,' he said.

I wished I hadn't told him that. Colin from The Lantern

Room had a really good part. He shouted all his lines standing with his feet together and his arms by his sides. You could hear him at the back.

I look into the empty restaurant through its little windows with the criss-cross lead on them like a Christmas card house, then I cross the road. It's only a bit further now to the police station.

There is an old blue lantern outside like the one on *Dixon of Dock Green* but the building is new. I have butterflies in my tummy as I walk up three steps to the door. It's made of glass and heavier than the doors at school. I manage to pull it open and go in. It's quiet, with grey walls and a light brown floor. There is a counter with a policeman behind it.

'Hello,' he says, 'are you lost?'

'No,' I say.

'How old are you?'

'Nine.'

'Where's your mum?'

'She's not here.'

'I can see that, where is she, though?'

'She died.'

He looks a bit annoyed that I've said that.

'Did she now?'

'Yes.'

'You sure about that?'

Does he think I'm making it up? No one's ever been like this before. But now I realise that I've never said out loud that Mum is dead. Everyone just knows. I think my class at school found out when Mrs Baker said: 'Just because your mother's died, there's no need to be spiteful.' That was on the stairs in the last year of infants.

'Why aren't you at school?' he says.

'It's finished.'

'Has it? What time is it?'

He looks up at a clock on the wall that shows it's half past three.

'Right, well, why have you wandered in here?'

'I want to tell you about my dad.'

'What about him?'

I look through the door behind him but I can't see anyone else. The policeman is resting his hands on the counter; I look down and push at the base of it with my shoe.

'One day he came into my room and made me take all my clothes off, then he got on the bed with me. He was only wearing his pants. We were on there for ages and he kept stroking me. His face was right up close to mine, it was rough and prickly, he was breathing in my ear. He was rubbing my bottom. I stayed still the whole time. Then he said this was our special cuddle and I must never tell anyone about this cuddle.'

I look up and he's staring at me.

'Hang on a minute, hang on, wait there,' he says.

He turns round to see if there is anyone else through the open door behind him but there isn't, so he moves to look for someone. He's saying something about a WPC. I look at a poster on the wall about men stealing car radios. Then an older policeman appears at the counter. He seems to be in charge.

'Tell the sergeant what you've just told me,' says the first one.

The sergeant has three stripes on his arm and a moustache, on his face.

'My dad came into my bedroom. It was the daytime. I don't know where my brother and sister were. He made me get undressed. Then he got on the bed with me. He was only wearing his pants. Then we lay on there for ages while he stroked me up and down. His face was scratchy and he was breathing on me. He kept rubbing my bottom. I couldn't move. He didn't say anything until the end when he said this was our special cuddle and I must never tell anyone about it.'

'But you're telling us?' says the sergeant.

'Yes.'

'Why?'

'I didn't like it, but I didn't want to tell my teacher.'

'Why not?'

'Because I like her.'

'Is your dad at home?'

'No, he's at work.'

'Do you know where he works?'

'Yes.'

'Well, tell us and we'll look up his phone number.'

'I know the number.'

'Do you?'

'Yes.'

'You're a clever boy, aren't you?'

It's true, I am clever, my nickname in class is Brainbox. I'm best at everything, apart from acting.

I tell him the number and he goes into the back room. I can hear the dial of a phone being turned. Then he comes back to ask my name and my dad's name. The first policeman offers me a packet of Garibaldi from behind the counter and I break off a piece. Then he has to get on with something. Two other policemen walk through. They look at me. I eat my biscuit. A man comes in to ask the policeman a question, I don't know what about, and he goes out again. Then the sergeant comes back.

'He'll be here to collect you in three-quarters of an hour.'

I look at him. The other policeman is looking at the clock as if he can't tell the time. I go towards the door.

'Hey, where do you think you're going? You wait there. Your dad is picking you up, and he's coming all the way from Liverpool Street so I shouldn't think he'll be too happy if you're not here when he gets here, do you?'

I turn to face him, my back to the door.

'You can sit over there.'

There is an orange plastic chair.

He bangs the packet of Garibaldi on top of the counter.

'Have another biscuit.'

He goes back through the door. I look at a poster about street crime. Once I saw a picture in the *Evening Standard* of a man in a grey suit being mugged in London. When Dad came home from work in his grey suit I started to cry. He asked me what the matter was and I told him about the man in the paper. He smiled and told me not to worry, no one was going to get Daddy.

The policeman at the counter is still pretending to be busy. I reach behind me to push open the heavy door and then I walk backwards outside. I go down the three steps, still backwards, and then walk backwards up Forest Road. I can see the police station going away from me as I make steady progress. The first policeman comes out of the door and looks around. I walk backwards behind a telegraph pole and stay still. After a moment I peek around the pole to see him but he's gone back inside.

I walk backwards past The Lantern Room and up to the crossroads, where I turn right, though it's on my left now, and continue to walk backwards up Staples Road.

I don't bump into anyone or anything. It's as if I'm

walking in a private version of the world where only I exist. I am all on my own and I don't mind. I know there is no one else here, so I don't feel lost or that there is someone I should be looking for.

I walk backwards up to the alleyway leading to The Drive and look at my Timex watch. It's almost half past three. I go home the normal way. I don't go to Forest Road. I don't go to the police station, I don't tell them anything, and they don't ring my dad at work.

When I'm nearly home I pass Luke's house. The front door is open. I can see Luke and his mum in the hall. They don't notice me. He is saying something to her and she says:

'Oh, leave me be, will you? Just leave me be.'

Scales

To be clear, that was a fantasy about Loughton Police Station that I had recently. At the time I wouldn't have dreamed of such a thing. I never went anywhere on the way home from primary school. It was almost a mile and a half to our house and I was expected in time for tea. Sometimes I might stop briefly at a newsagent where the urge to steal things was beginning to stir in me. I wanted so much of what I could see. I put a water pistol in my bag once but the man behind the counter saw me, so I said it must have fallen in. A likely story, and he'd seen me anyway. He said he'd decided *not* to call the police, which is the closest I came to the blue lantern as a boy. When he told me and Luke to 'go home', I felt a surge of relief within me that soon washed back and disappeared when I was outside in the calm water of Old Station Road. I resolved not to stop, but to improve, to become a better thief.

On days when I had a piano lesson I would go home to tea cooked by Jenny, our kindly tea lady, and then down the hill to my teacher Mr Clutterbuck's house. Then I'd come straight back for more Jenny-time and to wait for the phone to ring.

Dad would call every evening to say he was leaving to

come home. No one was tired or jaded about this call; it was always exciting when it came. And then to hear the keys in the door after he'd taken the train to Chingford from Liverpool Street, walked to his car and driven back to Loughton along Rangers Road. Did he fly down there at seventy or eighty? It was tempting on that long straight run with only the threat of deer crossing to worry you. Or did he dawdle along in no hurry to face the bedlam? He could have taken the Central Line in from Loughton but he preferred the Overground British Rail train that he'd been taking since he first went to work after he'd left school. The Underground trains had sprung seats that meant you were continually bucked into the air for the entire thirty-three-minute journey. It was almost impossible to read a book. Annoying as that was, I imagine he just preferred the routine. He took the same route to work every day of his working life until he retired at sixty-three, working for the one firm throughout, same firm, same route, same chair, same breakfast, same toothpaste, same soap, same everything, every day. With hindsight, I wonder if he was trying to impose structure on the turmoil of feelings and emotions suppressed inside, to control himself. So his hair never changed, his clothes never changed, his Toffos in the car, and his ancient tennis racket. Every year at the fair on Chingford Plain we went on the same rides, that he favoured, were forbidden from the rides he didn't like and then had to stand while he scored a maximum on the air rifle stall before claiming his prize, a box of Liquorice Allsorts, every time. His kids had to join the Cubs, and play cricket, and go to Bancroft's School, and he bought a little motorbike and little cars for them, because he loved motorbikes and cars (and hated giving lifts anywhere).

A few years ago, before I'd seen Dad's teen porn collection, I had a small reunion with one of my best friends from Bancroft's and my old girlfriend from Loughton College. We talked a little about my dad, who I notoriously could not get on with in those days. My ex-girlfriend rolled her eyes at the memory of it all and I tried to recall if I'd ever told her about the special cuddles, which stopped only four years before I met her. I muttered a derogatory remark about my father, something flippant about his meanness, and then my old friend said:

'Yeah, he only bought you a motorbike and a Mini 1275GT.'

And he stared at me, unsmiling, to let me know he knew who I really was, that I was lucky, and that I could scarcely have asked for more from the widower who brought three children up alone for ten exhausting years. It was true that I was given a 50cc Yamaha at sixteen, and then a car at seventeen, *but*, I thought, *you* were the one who said we should swap the wheels around on my Mini to even out tyre wear and after we'd done that the nearside front wheel came off and bounced over the kerb on to Chingford Plain and I had to look for it in the dark before being towed home by an AA truck the size of a fire engine (only with more flashing lights) and therefore could not keep it a secret from my dad who opened his bedroom window in his pyjamas, looked out at the light show and my gormless face blinking in and out of rotating amber, and shut the window behind him without a word. And also you don't know why my relationship with my dad was so bad because I never told you anything, you didn't know the truth and could only see two people at loggerheads, just an everyday father-and-son breakdown, and you ended up wondering why I didn't cut the poor sod some slack? And this was another effect of my abuse: people saw that we lived in a nice house and I went to a (fee-paying) public school and had a motorbike and a Mini, and naturally concluded that the problem must be mine. I was lazy at school, and stealing and smoking and vandalising, and, if anything, sympathy went to my dad. I often felt my friends didn't like me, and as I sat there with an old friend of thirty-something years that feeling returned, he didn't care for my views about my father, couldn't quite believe that I was still embittered and going on about him even though I was a father myself, and he didn't want to hear my complaints, which were evidence of my flawed character and reflected badly on me. There I was with a career I enjoyed, and a family and financial security, and there was my dad, who had recently turned eighty, pottering about with Alzheimer's, and hadn't I won? Didn't I have enough power now to lighten up and have a sense of humour about conflicts so far in the past? And still I couldn't say that, during our time together in the Lower Fourths, I was being abused by my father, and that as we were sitting there together I could picture me in the nude and Dad in his underpants and I didn't speak up because the padlock in my mind was locked and I did not have the key. I did not have power, I hadn't taken it, and it was still wielded over me in the form of a lifelong knot of silence.

Dad came home from work every evening looking tired and regretful that he had to open the front door. Every half-smile he wore appeared tainted by a twist of pain so we understood his life was hard and ours was frivolous joy. Even aged ten I could see there was some message of suffering being sent out and that my role, our role, was to quieten down, and not run up and hug him, not to touch him at all, so I would pull the *Evening Standard* out of his briefcase and look for the Closing Prices at the stock market as I knew they were important to Dad. We'd often see advertising for a big company and he'd say proudly: 'Got shares in them.' Then I'd turn to the cartoon strips.

On one occasion he pulled from his briefcase a small glossy magazine about *Starsky and Hutch*, my favourite TV show from which I learned much about the word on the street in downtown LA. I was thrilled, to have a gift, to be thought of, when the other two had nothing. It was a rare and wonderful moment. Perhaps we did have it easier than his generation who grew up during the Blitz.

He wouldn't ask if I'd been to my piano lesson and, understandably, he never wanted to hear me play. I assume our piano was an heirloom. It just appeared one day, upright, in dark wood with ornate knobs and decoration around the edges. Dad couldn't play a note, and would never try anything he couldn't do, to avoid looking silly, but he wanted us to learn. He also booked us in for ballroom dancing lessons as if we were being prepared for marriage in a Jane Austen novel (not that we had any of those in the house). Once the classes were reserved we forgot all about them and didn't go.

The piano had an opening above the keys where you could insert a roll of strong paper with holes in that resembled ancient parchment punctured with a secret code. Two big rectangular pedals came out on a hinge from within the bottom section and, by pedalling at the right speed, you could make the roll turn and the piano would play itself. Maintaining the right number of revolutions per minute seemed harder than learning the pieces yourself, and more fun was had playing too fast or too slow, which was when my sister and I began to laugh, causing Dad to intervene. Then it was back to practising scales. Mr Clutterbuck was big on scales.

There was a girl from my class at school called Ruth who had her piano lesson after mine. She had brown hair in a bob over her brown eyes and didn't say much, at least not to me, but I couldn't stop looking at her. One day for some reason she was waiting for her lesson in Mr Clutterbuck's piano room, rather than outside the door. Then Mr Clutterbuck (who reminded me of Mr Gruber in the *Paddington* books) asked me to sing a note, just an 'ah' sound. I dared not look round at Ruth. My face began to heat up. He played the note he wanted to hear. I croaked something out like a juvenile frog in the reeds. He was a patient old man and perhaps he hadn't noticed my mounting embarrassment, as my face turned more and more red. He hit the note again and I made another rainforest mating call. I enjoyed singing Christmas carols at school but I couldn't bear to sing alone and couldn't understand how so many of the groups on *Top of the Pop*s had male singers when no boys at my school would dream of doing that. Singing was something that girls did. I made one last strangled sound as if being pulled under by an anaconda, and he relented. I glanced at Ruth and, aged ten, experienced indifference in a woman for the first time.

One day, having dawdled along Loughton High Road, I realised I was going to be late for my lesson and went straight to Mr Clutterbuck's house. When I did eventually appear at home, Jenny had an unfamiliar pale look on her face. It hadn't occurred to me to ask Mr Clutterbuck to ring home for me. She said she'd assumed I'd gone to my lesson and was just pleased that I was home safely. After my mother died I began to have the feeling, which has carried into adulthood, that if I was absent I wouldn't be missed.

Just as I began to find my way around the piano keys and was being prepared for grade one, Mr Clutterbuck died. It was a terrible shame but to me, if anything, it felt reassuringly normal.

I remember he'd once shown a few of his pupils the church organ that he played at St Mary's. He let us push and pull the many knobs and press the pedals with our feet. He wanted to instil a love of music in us, but he'd gone too soon for me. A new piano teacher was found when I started at Bancroft's, but like most people there she seemed harsh and impatient. I thought she didn't like me, so I stopped music for life. Dad didn't seem bothered, and the Old Joanna fell silent.

Cigarettes

Granny Price came round once in the middle of the night. We were all upstairs in bed, in our separate rooms. My dad went to see who was at the door and found a lorry driver, who in turn had found Gran in the street, in her nightie. She'd asked him for a cigarette and said she wanted to go to our house.

That was what we were told by Dad. I don't know if he was in bed at the time or still up, only that it was The Middle Of The Night, which is a place defined by circumstances. If everyone is asleep in bed and it's dark and something happens, then that event is deemed to have taken place in The Middle Of The Night.

I'll arbitrarily assign the time of three o'clock. That may be an invention of mine or a half-memory created by something said long ago: 'It was *three o'clock* in the *morning*!' said Dad, or did he?

I was nine, or eight, I don't know, let's go with nine.

Perhaps Dad was waiting for his sleeping pill to counteract the Pro Plus he'd swallowed during the day, when the doorbell rang (or did they knock?). The lorry driver didn't come in. At least I didn't hear him, but then I didn't hear a lorry either. My bedroom was at the back of the house, and there was a driveway sloping down beyond the front steps to the road. Dad didn't invent the lorry driver, did he? No, he didn't invent things. He wasn't an imaginative parent. He didn't invite him in either, and I doubt he asked him to 'hang on', before disappearing back down the hall for a moment, only to return with a pound note in his hand 'for your trouble'.

He would likely have been irritated and embarrassed, possibly trying to share a look with the lorry driver, to find common ground in the face of typical stupidity from a woman, and hadn't they both seen plenty of *that* in their time? He'd have offered formal gratitude to the man (not an apology, not in his arsenal an apology) and seen him on his way.

So then it was Dad and his mother-in-law in the hall downstairs. They weren't the best of friends. I could hear talking but not what was being said. Gran was in no fit state to go home by the sound of it, but we didn't have a spare room.

It was over a mile from Gran's flat to our house. Where had she come across the lorry man, on Roding Road maybe? She must have been a sight in her nightwear, ghostly, adrift, about to be moved on by the wind like all the other uncared for detritus on the pavement that wafts in and out of the gutter, perilously close to the drains.

Gran hated cigarettes. They had killed Grandad Price, despite her futile efforts to keep him alive by not letting him smoke in the house. He smoked in the garden instead. Perhaps because he'd been a postman being outside was of no concern. I like to imagine him smoking on his round, even though I now know he worked at the Mount Pleasant sorting office. He didn't have much influence on our family, though he did make a doll's house for my sister, with working lights, and he built her a full-sized chest of drawers. My own daughter uses those drawers now, for all her little tops and bottoms. He died in 1974, less than two years after Mum. I wonder if her decline and death took a toll on him, the stress and the worry and the terrible pain of it. Did her illness shorten his life too?

Apart from the chest of drawers, the only thing of his I have is a tankard, which he'd won in his twenties, before the war, when he was a member of a rowing club in East London. The engraving reads:

C.S. REGATTA *PRESIDENTS EIGHTS* 1931
CRESCENT R.C F.C.PRICE (STR).

I presume the regatta was on the River Lea. I can't picture it. I don't know much about my mum's dad, I don't remember anything he said, but then, according to Granny, he didn't say much, especially in an argument, when he'd still his tongue completely: 'He was a *bugger*,' she told me.

And then he died, not long after their eldest girl, leaving no stories of her for us to cherish.

Their younger daughter, Hazel, had emigrated to Australia in 1963, with a husband and an eighteen-month-old son, and when Fred retired, he and Dolly sailed out to stay with them, to watch this brood of my distant cousins expand to four little people, toddling around Adelaide in the roasting heat. Granny only ever said that she didn't like the flies there, but they stayed for a year and a half.

'You went away for *eighteen months*!' Dad said to Granny after they came home. As if their trip was something that had happened to him, though for their part they must have wondered, as the boat pulled away from the quay to come home, if they'd ever see their youngest daughter and her children again. Dad couldn't show sympathy for the pain and the tears and the tearing apart of emigration. He wanted Granny nearby to help with his own recently arrived small children. But on their return they moved two hundred and sixty miles north to the seaside at Blackpool, where I enjoyed visiting them and playing in their pretty garden.

And then everything seismically collapsed. The emotional infrastructure of Granny's life went up in smoke, or was buried under a mudslide, or swept out to sea by a tsunami of loss, and virtually overnight she was in a wasteland of what had once been. When Mum died they came back from the Lancashire coast to a flat in Loughton, to help look after the three of us, their grandchildren here, and then Fred also died and Dolly was alone.

I don't know what year it was when Granny hitchhiked to our house, definitively I can only say between 1974, when her husband died, and 1979, when she left us. All that matters is that she was at her wits' end, defined as the end of her knowledge of herself, with no functioning faith to help her, hopelessly over-stretched, a piano wire of grief riddled with arthritis, tears constantly readying to tip out of her white-haired old head, flagging down a lorry driver to ask for a smoke. I expect he asked her something, since she wasn't quite litter yet, not dust yet. I wonder what he said?

a) 'You all right, love?'
b) 'Bloody hell, you must be freezing.'
c) 'What the hell are you doing?'
d) 'Mum? Oh Jesus, sorry, I thought you was my mum.'
e) 'Where do you think you're going?'

Or was she actually wandering dangerously in the road and he'd only just pulled up in time? Was she thumbing a ride from anyone who'd stop, with cars going by, and drivers thinking: 'Look at that mad old bat'?

'Old bat' can only mean a woman. It's derogatory, of course, arriving with us on a journey from the out-of-use term 'fly-by-nights', suggesting witchcraft, or its French equivalent, the Night Swallow (*hirondelle de nuit*), which implies prostitution. There are no nice terms for a woman out on her own at night.

Granny was not a witch or a prostitute. Though 'old bat' was widely used in the nineteen seventies, it didn't really mean those things any more, it was just a dismissive term for an elderly lady, a phrase running out of steam on its etymological route through the ages, powered by the mockery, ridicule and all-round subjugation of women for centuries.

Granny did use to know a couple of prostitutes, when she lived in a flat, presumably with Grandad before having children. These two women were in the flat upstairs and they had a lot of 'gentlemen callers'. She would have cups of tea with them around their kitchen table and their stories would make her laugh.

She wasn't laughing in our hall. Not with my dad.

Maybe she hadn't asked for a cigarette. Maybe the lorry driver was just smoking in the cab (everyone smoked then) and he offered her one. Maybe she'd locked herself out of the flat. Was she crying, sobbing, lost? Who was she looking for, her recently dead husband, her recently dead eldest daughter, her faraway youngest little girl?

She'd always had episodes, throughout her life, including postpartum depression. When she was up she was carefree, and when she was down she was hospitalised. Perhaps she was bi-polar, a modern term that wasn't in use then.

Why did she come to our house? Perhaps she'd forgotten Mum was dead. Perhaps we meant more to her than we realised. Grandchildren can't comprehend the deep blue love grandparents have for them, and the memories these little people evoke of the generation in between, who were also once small, curious, and alive.

No one said to us:

a) Your Granny loves you more than anything.
b) You're the only thing left to remind her of your dear mother.
c) Who she misses every day.
d) She is bereft.
e) She and your grandad were plucked from their happy retirement bungalow and travelled back to spartan accommodation by the M11 construction site, so they could help look after you.
f) And then Grandad died.
g) You're all she has.
h) Give her a kiss.
i) And a cuddle.
j) Tell her you love her.
k) Don't roll your eyes.
l) Don't answer back.
m) Eat up the dumplings she makes; years from now you'll wish for just one more bite of one.

Who might have said things like that? No one I knew.

No sooner had the lorry driver gone, than Dad and Gran were climbing the stairs. I would have had my usual toys for company in my bed, including the Dougal pyjama case that Gran had made for me. I don't remember showing any gratitude for that, even though I liked that my name was hand-stitched in red cotton lettering on its tail. It was too small to hold pyjamas, lacking the expansive capacity of, say, a snake. I still have it. I don't know if my brother still has his identical one. When Dad was on his way up it was often best to play dead. I lay in bed and kept quiet. I didn't go out to see Granny. I'm sorry, Granny. Had I appeared on the landing I might have jogged something in your mind.

He took her into his bedroom. It occurs to me now that she could have crept in to the spare single bed in my room, where she could have cried herself to sleep. Or maybe, had it been a couple of years later, we'd have opened the window and had a smoke together, since I was buying cigarettes (from the vending machine outside Loughton tube station) by age eleven. She might have told me something about my mum as she lit a fresh one from the end of the last. A few more years on and maybe she'd have pulled a quarter of Baileys from within her dressing gown and we'd have sipped from the bottle.

But the sleeping arrangements for the visitor were to be sharing a bed with my dad and there appeared to be some resistance next door. Gran was not a malleable individual. I remember her coming upstairs once looking for me because I'd upset my sister. I was hiding in the toilet.

'Where is he,' she said, 'hiding like a coward?'

I came out full of bravado, as if important pissing had been hurried to a conclusion, in order to face down this slur.

'Who's calling me a coward?' I declaimed (there were only the three of us there).

'I am!' she said, quivering slightly but used to a row, to standing her ground. I skulked off to my room.

When she was five Gran's father, Nelson Freeman, threw her mother, Fanny Binks, out of their house in Walthamstow. She never knew why. She described seeing her mum gazing at her in the school playground, from the other side of the gates. She looked away and when she looked back Fanny was gone, and never heard from again. Gran had older half-sisters from her dad's first marriage. They used to hit her on the head with a hairbrush, in lieu of bringing her up.

Now my dad was trying to persuade Gran out of her clothes, but wasn't she already in her nightie? I think I heard her say 'No' a few times, but she was confused and vulnerable or else she'd have fought him off more.

'Come on,' he said, 'take them off.'

Did he want to have *sex* with her? At the time I considered him to be lonely and sexually starved, which is how I explained his interest in the young skin beneath my pyjamas. But Gran's skin was dry and loose, and she was deranged, and unwilling. What was he doing?

'Take them *all* off.'

I knew that smothering tone, you're on your own, you may as well comply, you're cornered, no one can help you, no one will believe you, come on, why are you being silly? Your wishes are gone, do my bidding now, and after this you will always be diminished around me. I am clipping your wings, infusing you with Deep Shame. Take your clothes off.

Perhaps Granny and I were a threat. He could not fully control us; we were spirited, not compliant, often defiant. So he deployed his capacity for sexual deviancy to subjugate. He didn't want a fuck, he wanted silence. An unspoken arrangement that would function like a shackle, like a binding inside the head, a bond of repellent horror in a shared experience that would haunt us every day of our remaining lives.

I don't know what happened. Whether he undressed her. I fell asleep. Whatever it was I hope she forgot it, and the lorry driver, the cigarette, everything. It's what I wish for everyone with a dad like mine. Amnesia.

Other things must have happened after that night but I imagine the normal breakfast and going-to-school routines were observed the next morning, and nothing said.

The main consequence was that Granny was taken away for a while.

The hospital gardens were nice. There were lawns and flowerbeds. The grass sloped up to the main building, so famous in the area. On high ground, it could be seen from miles around with its tall chimney alongside a Gothic water tower. It was said that the chimney was there because they incinerated the bedding of the mad people after they died.

I couldn't see the chimney from inside my dad's car, though, or the tower, nor could I see any people from where we'd parked. I didn't dare unlock my door, I'd been told to stay put. Dad seemed genuinely to believe that there would be violent patients loose in the grounds prepared to harm a schoolboy. Although, had said boy unlocked his door and left the vehicle then he would *only have himself to blame.*

In fact, according to descriptions of the hospital I've since read, only the sick and infirm were near the public front entrance. Acute and chronic cases were kept much deeper inside.

I don't know where my brother and sister were that day, it was just me locked in the car. I didn't mind being alone, though I would have preferred to have an Enid Blyton with me, or a *Valiant*. Perhaps I did.

I was comfortable with solitude and familiar with the recurring feeling of being an inconvenience. It seemed a locked door between the world and me was the only satisfactory arrangement, though this rule did not apply to my bedroom.

The speedometer on the dashboard was dormant. It was my favourite feature of this car because it wasn't a dial. Speed was indicated by an orange line creeping along indicating 10, 20, 30, 40 miles an hour. It then crept back when you slowed down. But where did it go? It was as if it was retreating into a past that disappeared entirely, before the orange line darted out again with my dad's brown shoe leather on the pedal. It made the future seem exciting and the past traceless, lost, gone.

My dad liked a big family car, with a radio to listen to the cricket, brown vinyl seats, a fold-down armrest in the back, and no centre console under the dashboard so he could stretch his left leg out on longer drives. My mum was scared to drive the big car, preferring her Morris Minor.

She was once crawling along some Chingford side street in Dad's car, with the kids in the back, when the passenger door across from her swung open. She yelped in fear. Doors never opened when Dad was driving. Maybe it was a ghost getting in, a hitcher from the other side. You might think it would be her mum or dad, except they both outlived her. I wonder who it was. They didn't make a sound.

After half an hour or so in the car park I was bored. The windows were up but I don't remember it being hot.

Something on the radio would have passed the time, but also flattened the battery, and you wouldn't want to ask anyone round here for a push, never mind jump leads. I almost began to wish a crazy person would suddenly rattle the door handle. I knew Claybury was a 'loony bin' but Dad evidently thought no one was safe around here. Perhaps he was unconsciously leaving me there as a temptation. The nagging certainty that my absence improved his mood makes me think even now that he wouldn't have shed any tears if he'd returned to find me gone. I'd probably have 'unlocked the damn door'.

At my primary school we called people Claybury as an insult: 'you're a Claybury' or 'you're going to Claybury', or the pithy and to the point: '*CLAYBURY!*', which was said with the tongue pushed down behind the bottom lip to affect a speech impediment. This told the victim they were backward, stupid, destined for incarceration.

The original eighteenth-century Claybury Hall was converted, with new buildings added, to create an asylum for up to eight hundred male and twelve hundred female 'pauper lunatics', which tells you that a woman was at much greater risk of being certified insane. The hospital opened in 1893 and was the premier such facility of its time, sitting in fifty acres of gardens and surrounded by woodland. It also included a huge laundry that washed for operating theatres all over London. Now my Gran was in there, following her excursion to our house in the Middle Of The Night.

I didn't see my dad approach when he came out. He was a rapid pedestrian and had the driver's door open before I could ready myself to please him. I tried to wear an expression of mild curiosity but I knew he would be impenetrable from the look on his face. We swung around and down the hill out of the car park. That was my only visit.

I wondered if my dad wished that his deceased wife's ailing mother should also be dead. Surprisingly the Greeks don't seem to have had a specific word for that. There is geronticide, the abandonment of an elderly person to die, or senicide, the killing of the elderly who have become a burden (or a 'bit of a worry' we might have said). Given how lauded Captain Oates was during my childhood, for selflessly exiting the doomed Scott expedition to the South Pole sixty years previously, it might be presumed of any English person, who had become a bit of a worry, that they would opt for posthumous reverence by doing the decent thing, perhaps availing themselves of a discreetly placed Baileys and a revolver. Most humans don't have the option to just wander out into the forest and lie down like a tooth-less old badger or a wolf, and those mammals don't have teams of their kind running facilities to aid their improba-ble return to health, or else ease their slow decline.

It was made clear, with every tight-lipped silence, that all this was difficult for Dad. Perhaps more so for him than for Gran, given that *he* hadn't caused it, he hadn't shown weakness, *she* had. It was as if it was happening to him. He wasn't one for empathy. Had he been he might have found a way to explain to me, on the return journey, what was happening to Granny and how long she might be there and why I couldn't see her, before he released me from the car.

At home the feeling among the grandchildren (without learned life skills like sympathy or kindness) was an unspo-ken consensus that Granny would be better off dead. She was annoying, and Dad was under enough stress as it was. Given her skeletal craziness, perhaps she would die now anyway, and we might all get a little kickback from Dad's relief after the event.

But while we were waiting for her to die, she emigrated.

She went to live in Australia with our auntie, who once sent me felt tips for a birthday. She was so reduced by then she may have quietly boarded as a stowaway, carried by sympathetic rodents up a mooring rope. Her surviving daughter fattened her into a sphere, a rotund, chuckling songbird, occupying a backyard extension where she eked out sixteen more years.

On my first trip to see her, with my sister, in 1988, Gran told me about my dad's Claybury visit. She said he'd stood at the end of her bed (not at the bedside I noted, not holding her hand, not sitting for a while) and said:

'Complete breakdown, mental and physical.'

As if it were a weakness on her part.

'As if I'd failed,' she said.

It was on that trip, during one of the many conversations we had about the past, that I told her about Dad coming into my room at night and making me undress. She said that perhaps he was just cuddling me to make sure I was all right, after our mum had died. I couldn't persuade her from that point of view and eventually gave up. I didn't ask her about the lorry man, or the cigarette, or my dad's bedroom.

I went to visit her on three more occasions. In March 1992 she was in an Adelaide psychiatric hospital staring out of the window when I arrived. By chance it was my birthday. I was turning twenty-six. In the past she might have given me half a re-used birthday card, with a greeting scrawled on the back of the torn-off picture, but she was motionless and didn't acknowledge me.

Talking to my Australian cousins I learned that, in the

past, she had wandered off and been brought home in her nightie there too. Now my aunt told me that, since Granny was depressed, not eating, and could well make herself die, the doctors were going to use electric shock treatment on her, and that it wouldn't be the first time she'd had it.

Electroconvulsive Therapy is still used, nowadays under a general anaesthetic. You're twice as likely to have it as a woman than as a man.

I went to see her the day after they'd passed a current through her. She was sitting with other patients, busily eating baked beans with a pink plastic spoon from a lime-green plastic bowl, held in the palm of her shaking hand.

I felt she was the most important person in my life. All I had. I hoped my being there gave her a little strength, and that she felt the love I wanted to give her, since I couldn't find the words, couldn't find a hug.

'They zapped me, Alan,' she said.

'I know, Gran. I'm sorry.'

'I don't like it.'

'It's worked, though, Gran. It's nice to see you eating,' I said.

She conceded with a sigh and with evident reservations. Then her watery eyes looked up at me like those of a small mammal recently released from a trap, but not yet strong enough to run.

Animals

Grandpa Davies came with us when we went to Chessington Zoo, perhaps because Granny Davies had passed away by then, which would put that trip into the summer of 1975. I was nine.

It must have taken at least an hour and a half to drive there from Essex, the windows down all the way and probably Test Match cricket on the radio, with Dennis Lillee and Jeff Thomson terrorising English batsmen as Australia's fast bowling attack. Now we were at last out of the car and disinterestedly ambling along crowded paths. There was a fork ahead. I went left while my father, grandfather, brother and sister went right. I was being playful; it looked as though the paths joined up a little further ahead, beyond a sort of island covered with bushes and shrubbery. I went out of sight, pleased with my derring-do, trying to buck the day up a bit, generate a bit of excitement. Then I realised that the paths didn't connect up again, and I couldn't see my family and I was lost.

My lungs felt as though they were deciding whether they could carry on, then panic turned up and I faltered at the first choice: go back or carry on. I was afraid to move, I tried to occupy the smallest space I could and then the

fear of being found took hold; it could be worse than being
lost. Naturally, it didn't occur to me to ask anyone for help.

Throughout my childhood I felt I was never more than
seconds away from irritating the family, causing them to
unite wearily, then they'd raise the drawbridge and I'd be
outside the walls again. Usually I could annoy them by
accident; I didn't even have to try. I tried not to, in fact.

I was eventually found, or come across, as suddenly as I'd
inadvertently given them the slip. There were no smiles. I
gravitated towards Grandpa Davies and the rest of the visit
passed in near silence, our solemn faces not unlike those
of the penned animals. Later I saw a goat that had escaped
from a petting area and was being led back. The keeper
said: 'He does it all the time.'

Grandpa also came with us to the Isle of Man for the TT
races. I'd normally be seated next to Dad on a trip but I
had to squeeze into the back seat next to my siblings when
Grandpa joined us. I read paperbacks the whole time. I
took twelve with me on holiday in my new Arsenal shoulder bag (which I still have), but I couldn't read on the Isle
of Man with the motorbikes going past, it was too exciting,
especially the sidecars with their daredevil passengers. Dad
eulogised constantly about the aroma of Castrol racing oil.
It was sweet smelling, as if honey had been added to the
fuel tanks of two-stroke machines, whose high-revving
engines buzzed past like a swarm of numbered bees.

I did manage to read *Black Beauty* in the back of the car,
ploughing through it, engrossed. The narrator (a horse,
of course) had such humility, loyalty and courage that he
endeared himself to millions. Children often enjoy books
about good people, preferring villains to see the error of
their ways. Only adults like their protagonists cynical,

vain and cruel. Kids like nice people, preferably with a sweet tooth, and clumsy bears, and spirited dogs who save drowning children, cats who can't catch birds, and noble horses. They are open-minded, able to believe even in a miraculous healer of the sick, a feeder of the starving, who cares not for possessions but only for all things bright and beautiful and who would, for the common good, make the ultimate sacrifice. Like Black Beauty nearly had to, before finding peaceful retirement in a heavenly grassy field.

Grandpa took me to Trafalgar Square a couple of times, just us, with him holding on to the hood of my parka so as not to lose me in the crowds. Then he'd buy bird seed from a vendor near the lions at the foot of Nelson's Column, and up to eight pigeons would settle on me as I stood like a reverse scarecrow, with tempting kernels along my arms and on my head. Grandpa didn't put any seed on his own bald bonce (as he might say), so no birds alighted among the wisps of white hair or perched on his wire-rimmed glasses. He stood with his feet together smiling benignly at my delighted face. Every so often a car would backfire and every pigeon in the square flew off at once. For lunch he'd take me to J. Lyon's Tea Room (now a Pizza Express) on The Strand where I'd have pork chops. He referred to it as 'Jo Lyon's'. Perhaps he knew the founder, as I subsequently learned that during the fifties he'd run The Talbot, a similarly busy restaurant in the City of London. He was mild and kind. Only once did he show irritation with me. It was at our dining-room table. Dad had gone out of the room, so it was just him and the three children. He held me by the wrist with surprising force, I've no idea what I'd done, but he felt the need to restrain me. On a similar occasion, though, he stuck up for me when my father yelled my name from the kitchen over some dust-up that was actually between my brother and sister. He'd had brothers; I think they died in World War One.

His wife, Granny Davies, often used to say to me: 'What are we going to do with you?' But he never said that, he left me alone.

We would take the tube from Charing Cross back to Loughton and I would look for his old Wolseley in the car park. It was a mauve and grey two-tone affair with chrome trim and bumpers. Small and brimming with character, if it had worn a hat it would have tipped it at passers-by.

And its lights were on, so the battery was flat.

Someone came to collect us. Amid the adult muttering and bickering, I sat silently in the back, on a bouncy seat with actual springs in.

Towards the end of his life I suggested to my sister, with a characteristic lack of empathy, that Grandpa would be better off dead. We'd never seen him being sprightly, but now he was just sleepy, and he had difficulty chewing his food, which must have embarrassed him. We didn't know about the thriving restaurant he used to run with hundreds of covers every lunchtime and Freemasons meeting in the basement, or how he'd helped to build the Scout hut where my parents used to meet, when Mum was looking for a husband and Dad was looking for ... who knows what?

And we didn't know he had Parkinson's.

One Sunday at our house, Grandpa pulled himself out of his armchair in front of the cricket, and disappeared quietly into our recently completed downstairs cloakroom, which featured a turquoise lavatory and shower tray. Then I heard my dad call out: 'Alan, will you come in here, please?'

My brother or my sister were nearby, but not required.

Unusually, a job had come up for which I was the best candidate. I crossed the hall from the living room into the new toilet at the foot of the stairs. My father and his father were standing around the bowl. My dad asked me to help Grandpa and then slipped out without another word.

Grandpa by now was struggling with his balance and the use of his hands, which he'd placed against the walls to support him. His penis was sticking out of the front of his big brown trousers. It had the look of an uncooked spring roll. There was silence. I reached over and held it in my twelve-year-old fingers, not tightly, just enough to help him take aim, and we stood there as he went. Then I put it away, helped him with his fly and left him alone.

I suppose Grandpa had called out for his son and when Dad saw him there, wrestling with Parkinson's and doubtless feeling ashamed, he had chosen to delegate to me. It felt connected to our own intimate relations somehow. Why he didn't do it himself is lost between him and his dad.

Pants

My Y-fronts were full of shit. Dried out by my body temperature and pancaked by my weight (about four stone or twenty-five kilos for an eight-year-old), it was now squashed down into a mould of my young boy's bottom as I sat in the car.

No one else knew it was there, so if I behaved as though waiting normally in the back seat it could yet remain a secret. I had learned that it's sometimes nice to share secrets, but usually best to keep them. Once I was home I could deal with the (faecal) matter privately. The car was white but the interior seats were charcoal, or *gris foncé*, or lunar dusk, or whatever term a car manufacturer would use, so if anything seeped out it shouldn't be visible.

Earlier, I had stayed in the car while the rest of the family went to a nearby attraction. I forget what it was, only that we had been motoring around long enough to get on each other's nerves. A joyless atmosphere was pushing at the windows to escape by the time Dad parked the car, reversing into a spot with his tongue habitually sticking out as he turned to see behind.

It didn't appear that way but when I refused to budge from my seat I was actually reaching for him, a small boy's hand stretched out. If I sit here and don't move he'll have to listen to me, to sympathise, empathise, consider my feelings and show kindness, love even, towards his second child. Or at least make eye contact. The other two can amuse themselves in the car park for a minute while we make a special connection, father and most troubled son.

Oh, he's gone.

For a while it was enjoyable in there, or anywhere, on my own. I moved into Dad's seat behind the black steering wheel and imagined driving. There were three pedals below and I tried to reach them with my inexpensive, unbranded trainers but it was difficult to do that while looking out of the windscreen, my head sank down behind the dashboard as my toes brushed the accelerator and the brake and whatever that one on the left was.

Then I noticed that the keys were in the ignition. Dad had left an unlocked car with the keys in it, normally the fastest way to have your vehicle taken if you are plotting a bogus insurance claim. But was it the car he wanted taking away? It didn't occur to me until now that he might have wanted me to be stolen, and I don't think it occurred to him, either, at least not consciously.

I saw it as an opportunity to try driving.

Holding the steering wheel with my free hand I turned the key, as I'd seen Dad do hundreds of times. There was some noise from under the bonnet as the starter motor drew power from the battery and tried to fire up the spark plugs. The Triumph Dolomite was a sporty-looking car, designed by Giovanni Michelotti who crafted many beautiful Ferraris and Maseratis. As I turned the key it felt as though something momentous was going to happen. The engine turned over and the car lurched forward, bucking me out of my seat, as it seemed to prepare itself for a journey on its own terms like something from a Stephen King novel. And then, no sooner had it come to life than it shuddered into stillness. I was relieved. I had thought it was going to bolt across the car park.

I realised years later the car had been left in gear. Even though we were parked on the flat, no one trusted hand-brakes in those days, so this was sound practice. Being safety-conscious enough to leave his car in first, while at the same time leaving a child inside and the keys in the ignition, is the kind of seeming contradiction that makes Dad so *fascinating*.

I retreated to the back seat and settled below the windows, relieved that my family hadn't seen the incident. Hindsight suggests that movement in my bowels may have begun as a consequence of turning the key. I was often caught short in this way, as if I lacked a conventional early-warning system, causing crisis situations, usually resolved by finding a toilet in the nick of time. But on this occasion I was afraid to leave the car to look for a public convenience. Other anxieties were also in play, being abandoned by my father for one, which might have pushed imminent defecation down the pecking order of concern.

The feeling of not being able to stem the tide was familiar, perhaps even comforting. Though I didn't think my Y-fronts could be breached, I had still only allowed it out slowly, with controlled reluctance, as if filling my underwear with Play-Doh being squeezed through a toy ice-cream maker. It emerged only because my body could safely contain it no longer. Although compacted hard waste in your rectal cavity is not life threatening, pushing it out can be. Straining breathlessly can lower blood pressure and trigger fatal heart arrhythmias, though how many children have died from cardiac arrest while trying not to soil their dad's new car I don't actually know. Without any pre-existing congenital heart defect I was probably safe.

In any event I shat myself. And then I waited.

In our back garden at home Dad had netting put up behind our goalposts to protect Mum's rose bushes. One night a hedgehog became caught up in it. It was difficult to release as it kept rolling into a ball, taking the tangled net with it. My dad suggested putting a saucer of milk down and leaving it alone. I now know that milk gives hedgehogs diarrhoea, so it was in for a long night, both caught in a trap and soiling itself.

I pulled my shorts down far enough to peer in to my St Michael underpants and saw they had held. An outstanding brand, they are the first port of call for the incontinent child. I knew a crust would form on the surface, and as my balls were undescended and my penis had been a slow starter, there was room in there for this cowpat, which would soon resemble the fossilised footprint of a long extinct proboscidean.

It was some time before my family came back. The faeces had dried out and I was confident it was undetectable. I saw them on the other side of the car park before they saw me, and watched their approach with some relief. I'd felt lonely. Shitting yourself takes the edge off 'me time'.

They looked happy. I resolved to act out some version of events in which staying in a car on my own was not just what I wanted to do, it was what any intelligent person would choose, rather than be out in the sunshine eating ice cream.

My five-year-old sister came to my side of the car. I could

just see the top of her head through the window as she reached for the handle. She pulled the door open to reveal her smiling face, I smiled back, and her look instantly changed into one of startled disgust, before she reeled backwards with her hand over her mouth.

'He's pooed himself!' she said.

I could see my dad's face outside the car, the shock and the beginnings of anger. A look that said this too had better not get out, another secret.

My brother opened the door on the other side.

'He has, he stinks!'

They all stood back, making what I considered to be a lot of it, with exaggerated gestures of revulsion and unnecessary retching noises. But then I hadn't thought to wind down a window, so a lot of invisible gas must have plumed out.

I suppose the pants went into a bin. I would then have sat in my shorts, all the way home, and probably acted as if everything was normal, which it was, in a way.

It was a few years before I had a similar catastrophe. In some ways it was worse because I was eleven, a bit big for an accident in my trousers.

We were on holiday in Newquay and things were less than harmonious. Each evening Dad liked us all to put on our best clothes for dinner and brush our hair neatly. My brother became so incensed waiting for me, as I stood in front of the mirror creating a centre parting like Kid Jensen's on *Top of the Pops*, that he kicked me hard in the leg. Dad sent him to the sin-bin of the hotel corridor, while I carried on combing with affected nonchalance to hide the pain. It was unusual for my brother's mask to slip. The scales of our mutual loathing were tipping and his was the weightier side. But I don't know if it was family tension that unsettled me that day or if I just had an upset tummy.

We went down for dinner in the hotel restaurant (bottle of squash marked with a biro and left with the waiter) and I immediately needed the toilet. Dad sent me off saying I should have gone beforehand. The only WC I knew of was occupied, and someone was waiting. I moved urgently through the corridors, not asking for help and oblivious to a large Gents close by, and then, despite an ahead-of-my-years centre parting, I defecated in my Best Trousers. I wasn't Kid Jensen after all, just a kid.

I don't remember how I broke the news, or whether everyone finished their meals double-quick, or if one of them had come to look for me, but the shame sank in during the long silence back in our room as Dad washed out my wool–polyester mix trousers in the sink. A task he did not pretend to enjoy. I wanted him to chuck them out, they had a hideous grey checked pattern and I hated them, detracting as they did from my excellent hairstyle.

When boys soil themselves there are supposedly underlying psychological factors at work, in addition to poor time and distance management. Among the primary causes of erratic bowel control are:

1. Fear of the toilet.
2. Stressful life experiences such as bereavement or sexual abuse.
3. Anal fissure.

Given number two, it's a miracle I didn't number two myself more often. Number one does not apply. I love the toilet; to this day it's where I find myself when I'm feeling anxious, probably because it was the only room in my child-hood home with a lock on it. I don't understand the third one and I'm not prepared to type it into a search bar even with an activated family filter.

On one occasion as a boy I managed to soil a pair of my Y-fronts in my own home. I was too ashamed to tell anyone, so I went into the front garden and buried them in the flowerbed next to the wall by the road. They were an old white pair. I'd had them for years. For days I couldn't stop thinking about them out there, so I went to check on them one night by torchlight and I had cause to regret the shallow grave I'd dug as they'd been removed. I knew it was my dad who must have found them and, though he never said anything, I knew he'd know they were mine. My name was sewn in the back of them.

As I'd hoped, nothing was ever said about those buried Y-fronts. The memory of them came to mind when I was driving through the Essex countryside, with Dad's pictures next to me, including those of him in his own secret pants.

After I had pulled over by a field to look through them, I drove out to the crematorium where my mum's ashes were buried. It was further than I thought, I was a little lost, but eventually I found the entrance and the car park. I walked up into the woods behind the crematorium. Everything looked different from my last visit. Many more memorial benches and posts with various plaques on had appeared; there were fresh flowers everywhere, perhaps because it was June. Several saplings had flourished in a new section of woodland. I'd gone quite far along a winding path when I realised I needed the toilet.

Looking behind me I could see a hearse just pulling up outside the crematorium with crowds of people arriving from the car park beyond, and I didn't want to intrude. I picked my way rapidly into a narrow space between young trees, well away from the various pots and vases marking buried urns, to a shaded spot where it was quiet and I could be neither seen nor heard. There I released a considerable spring into the summer air. Fortunately it was only my bladder that was in need of relief, but after several seconds I wondered if this flow would ever stop. I couldn't speed it up, as it emerged with all the velocity of an elderly person with a walking frame on a zebra crossing. In mid-stream I wondered about scattered ashes beneath my feet and the shame of being found doing this over someone's grave. On one visit to this place several years before, I'd turned up on a motorbike and kept my helmet on as it was raining. A woman had fled the memorial woods at the sight of me. The next thing I knew a police dog handler was demanding I remove my helmet while his German shepherd eyed me up. People could become quite jumpy in these places. Emotions might surface in unexpected ways. But: 'Remove your helmet, please, sir' was preferable to: 'If you could stop relieving yourself upon the deceased, please, sir.'

The trees were too narrow to hide behind, and I was in my early fifties so every passing of fluid could break up into a three-part mini-series. I had to shuffle slightly to the side when I realised I had aimed uphill and the firm summer ground had rejected my offering. It was pooling in front of me hesitantly and now began to turn back the way it had come, as if heading for the source, eventually rushing between my feet, which were now unnaturally far apart. I began to fear cramp in my toes and was grimacing in a way not often seen in a garden of rest. 'Please,' I said, 'please, please, please.' Finally it was over. I scanned the woods, hoping I hadn't been heard, at least not by a mortal, and to satisfy myself that I was not guilty of violating anyone's lasting peace. I was beyond the perimeter and had been alone throughout, apart from witnesses from the spirit world, of course. After a minute or two to calm down, I rang my sister.

A few years before, after Uncle Pat's funeral at the same place, Dad had spotted a middle-aged woman among the mourners and asked my stepmother who it was. My sister was shaken to learn her father hadn't recognised her. A diagnosis of Alzheimer's followed, the same condition that had ruined his brother's last years.

My sister and I spoke on the phone for longer than we had in quite a while, about our mum, our stepmother, our father, and what to do with unwanted hardcore pornography.

'My dad's a paedophile,' she said, 'I can't believe it.'

She thought it best to throw the rest of his pictures away. Keep it all a secret.

'Go back to your family,' she said, 'he'll be dead soon.'

We agreed to keep in touch.

When I arrived home from the crematorium, which is about an hour's drive away, I sat in the car outside my house for a while. My wife, of ten years by then, was inside and so were our three children. I looked out through my windscreen at the big green recycling bin on our front path, knowing I could drop the whole folder in there and it would be taken away by the council.

I pulled out the four photos of my children's grandpa in his briefs. Should I just chuck them? Why had my step-mother given them to me? Did she want something to happen to him? Or me? Should I keep his embarrassing underwear a secret as he had mine?

One pair of my dad's skimpy undies was comparable to the red knickers that Superman wears over his leotard, not quite a posing pouch or a thong but they didn't look designed for comfort during a hard day's chartered accountancy. Whether the others were similarly inadequate, or provocative, is in the eye of the beholder, I suppose, or whoever it was behind the viewfinder.

Rather than bury them in the front garden, I decided to take those four pictures of Dad into the house and hide them, but I didn't know what to do with the rest of his collection. I wasn't sure if I was committing an offence just by carrying them around and looking at them. Were these kids minors?

My wife knew what I had gone to collect from my stepmother and we agreed that we didn't want it in the house, partly in case our children came across it. They were all far too young for us to explain that this is what half-hearted sodomy and coerced fellatio look like. I decided to put the PG Tips carrier bag under the floor mat in the passenger footwell of my car, and went indoors.

I then spent the night worrying about the car being stolen.

The next day I took the package from its hiding place and, rather than drop it in the recycling bin, took it to my lawyer's office. She is someone I've known and trusted for some time. I told her all about my father and what had happened to the little boy in his care. My lawyer has a little boy of her own and I noticed there were tears filling her eyes, and then tears filled mine, and we composed ourselves and she asked me what I wanted to do. I said I wasn't sure. She agreed to store the pictures in a file at her firm's offices. It would be labelled as pertaining to me but as my father's collection, not mine, should that ever need clarifying. I wanted time to think.

The four pictures of my dad in his undies were hidden in a drawer at home. Another of his secrets was safe with me. For the time being.

Exams

There are several possible reasons why I was still wearing the Y-fronts of a six-year-old at age eleven:

1. I could still get them on.
2. They were from the durable Marks & Spencer St Michael range.
3. They were not being unduly strained by descending testicles.
4. Dad didn't buy anything unless he absolutely had to.
5. Mum had sewn my name in the back of them so they were precious.

When I started at secondary school all the Y-fronts in our house, including Dad's, were white, which would still have been Mum's choice. I learned years later that well into his twenties Dad's clothes were laid out for him each morning by his mum. Then my mum took over and did everything for him, while he checked the tyre pressures on the car, mowed the lawn and tried to keep our left elbows high during forward defensive shots.

When Mum was in hospital, she asked me if I would help

Dad with sorting out the washing at home. He always seemed amazed that I knew which things were mine and which were my brother's. It was exciting to be a valued helper. This was what primary school felt like, tasks I could do and enjoy, with praise and encouragement flowing. I was six.

Dad's pants were easy to spot, they were massive and had no name tag. Plus there was the skiddage, the skiddery, the skidarama. I used to read *Tiger* and one of the comic strips starred Formula One driver Skid Solo. He would come to mind on washday. No detergent on the market could wash out my father's blemishes but nothing could persuade him to buy new pants, or laundry bleach, which makes me wonder if those bright little panties he squeezed into for some photographs were actually a gift.

So, like my dad, I'd had the same underpants for years, and no one was interested in them, but that changed at secondary school where it was mandatory, as established by an Act of Parliament in 1907, that all boys had a medical examination.

I was a year younger than the others, more than that in most cases, which was often a problem but never more so than during my examination when I found myself on the wrong side of the puberty divide. Afterwards, a group of us stood around the locker room talking about the medical.

'What about when they made you get on that bed?' I said. 'It was so high I nearly couldn't get up there!'

'What bed?' said one of them.

Five or six unsmiling thirteen-year-old faces looked at me. I was eleven.

'What bed?' said another.

Two more piped up.

'I didn't have to go on no bed.'

'I never got on a bed.'

If any of them actually had been asked to get on the bed they weren't going to say so now, not with the way the wind was blowing.

'What did they do, then?'

'What?' I said.

The locker-room ceiling seemed unusually low, its bare brick walls and cold stone floor particularly unforgiving. The lockers had grey metal doors with padlocks, concealing wire cages where wet towels and textbooks covered in wallpaper came together. The further in you went the older the boys became, so venturing all the way to the back was unadvisable.

I was desperate for someone to change the subject. Why did I try to join in the conversation in the first place? To raise a smile? Would I never learn? Instead, I was now vulnerable to their sardonic, adolescent cool.

'No one went on any bed except you.'

'It was just part of the medical,' I said.

'No it wasn't.'

Facing my locker to hide my blushes I put my hand in my pocket and felt the small red plastic dragon that I always carried with me (as a mascot, charm, friend). Carefully not letting them see my little toy, I pulled out the key for my padlock, revealing the keychain that was fixed to my waistband, another of Dad's ideas that, like the saddlebag on my bike, invited mockery. At least it took their minds off my medical. When the scrum half of the rugby team yanked on it so hard that it snapped I couldn't pretend to be annoyed.

The doctor had spent quite a long time examining my genitals, was what I couldn't bring myself to say. This was done unsympathetically, as if I was a nuisance. The embarrassment! It would have been better to faint like a first year at the front of assembly during Prize Day rehearsals. Thud, there goes another, then some shuffling while they are taken out.

I didn't dare to speak as I lay there on my back with my head turned to face the wall. Rising anxiety soon made it hard to breathe normally and to top it all it seemed both Matron and the doctor disapproved of my penis.

Matron was doubtless itching to put some iodine on it.

Time slowed, then it stood still, and then seemingly slipped back from 1978 when I had come in, to 1928 judging by Matron's uniform, to what might have been 1878 when I looked at the stone walls around me. Cold, clammy fingers continued to lift, push and turn my shrunken appendage. This was the first indication I'd had that all was not right down there, though they did not explain what they were looking for. That would have amounted to reassurance, which was anathema to them, a sign of weakness that might spread like a contagion to the boys. If the doctor had said: 'He's beyond help, Matron, pass my revolver,' it would have been unsurprising to be part of a secret atrocity and buried at the bottom of the field, only for my bones to be discovered a hundred years later, during the building of a launch pad for the new school rocket.

I was behind in my development. I hadn't dropped yet, but I was younger than the other boys, I shouldn't have been in that year at all. I was born in March '66 and some of them were September or October '64. Several in the year below were older than I was, never mind *everyone* in my year.

I'd been moved up, out of Staples Road primary school, where I was thriving, and into Bancroft's, with its Latin,

Rugby and Combined Cadet Force. It was my dad's old public school so I had to pretend I wanted to be there, even though my testes were behaving as if it was 1973 and they were still at primary.

My father was informed that my age-six Y-fronts were hindering my genital growth. Ironically, that sounded like bollocks, but he believed everything that came from the school, as if they could never be mistaken or unjust. I felt they were routinely both.

Dad explained the pants situation to me in a kind voice. Maybe he combined the news with a little molestation as it was only then that he spoke softly to me. At other times he was short-tempered, but he had a lifetime pass to behave as he wanted, because he had been:

Left Alone With Three Small Children and It Must Be Very Hard For Him.

That was, I learned, his situation as seen from the outside, and it trumped all my complaints about him to others. Although I kept the most significant cause for complaint to myself, never mentioning that being alone was affording him all sorts of opportunities as he tiptoed between his bedroom and mine.

With hindsight, boarding at the school might have been safer for me, but I never wished I was a boarder, only that home life might improve. It was also common knowledge that boarders were at the mercy of one of the teachers who lived there, and who walked about half-naked in a bath-robe that could not stay tied up *no matter what he did*. We believed this rumour about him because we'd seen him pick his nose and eat it during a lesson and it felt a short jump from there to other depravity.

That Mum had died four years before was perhaps one of

the reasons I was put up a year. With my brother already at Bancroft's and my sister at the girls' primary down the road, it meant three kids in three different places each morning and if I could go on the bus with my brother, life would be simpler for Dad, who had been:

Left Alone With Three Small Children and It Must Be Very Hard For Him.

I was considered academically up to it; my nickname was Brainbox, after all. Whether I was emotionally and physically ready, given that I had recently lost my mother and had dormant genitalia, was not discussed.

I was thriving at Staples Road County Primary in the care of Mrs Thorogood. Although when she had become our teacher in the third year (now known as Year 5), I had become disruptive. I had a habit of repeating things she said to amuse my friends, though it was transparently an attempt to draw attention to myself. A needy little boy sitting near the back.

One day she spent a long time filling the blackboard with writing and then had to leave the room. I took the board rubber, went to the front, and wiped out the bottom sentence while the rest of the class looked on in disbelief.

When she came back in she asked who had done it and I immediately confessed. She told me off but at least I'd caught her eye.

One morning, soon after that, as the class went out into the corridor to go down to the hall for assembly she asked me to stay behind. I was pleased, as this was the first evidence that I had a unique relationship with her. Secret time alone, I had learned, was the way to form a bond with a significant adult. Now she would confirm that I was the most special child in the third year.

She asked why I repeated everything she said. I couldn't find an answer, lacking the wit to repeat the question. I smiled but she did not. In fact, she looked distressed, and as I look back I realise that she was twenty-three, just out of teacher training, I was her first problem child, and perhaps it was the part of the job she dreaded the most.

I started crying, which took us both by surprise. She could tell I wasn't pretending, I couldn't stop, if anything I went up a gear, and became loud and snotty, and then I was shaking, and I kept saying sorry, and she must have thought she'd made the wrong call, that keeping me back had been a disaster and what if the headmaster went by and saw his new member of staff with the boy whose mum had died from leukaemia and he was bawling his eyes out as if she was tormenting him in a one-to-one punishment session. Perhaps she was thinking: 'Please stop crying, please, please, someone will see us.'

But she didn't say anything like that. She was comforting and gave me a cuddle, which I'd been a bit short of for a while, and I subsided and we became friends. It was as if she'd watered me and put me in the sun. We are still friends today.

Mrs Thorogood changed into a tracksuit for PE. I raced her up the playground and back and I won, because she slipped when we turned, and because I was the fastest in the class.

Mrs Thorogood wore a swimming costume and came into Loughton Pool with us when we had a lesson. The boys jumped in and chased her. I went under the water and made a grab for her thigh, slightly pinching it. She told us that that was *enough* and to go to the side, so we did and she got out.

Mrs Thorogood divided us into teams and awarded merit marks. My team was called *The Brady Bunch* after the American TV show and also, for me, because Liam Brady was playing for Arsenal. He was nineteen at the time and becoming my idol. Our team scored more merit marks than any other.

One day we had a Big Test, with a variety of questions, arithmetic and spellings among them. I scored forty out of forty. A couple of kids were in the thirties, most in the twenties. I was the cleverest, the best at football (apart from a boy who was new so didn't count) and the fastest. I was good at rounders, I won the high jump, I was even in the lead-off pair for country dancing with Nicola Rabey.

When my father told me that I could go to his old school the next year it was presented to me as if I'd won the lottery. I was going to have to take a little test at Bancroft's but it was seemingly a formality.

The day came and my dad took me up to the place I knew he loved the most, an imposing Victorian red-brick building in Woodford next to Epping Forest. The entrance is a tower with large wooden gates, with a smaller gate inset so that you pass through into the quadrangle with its immaculate grass where masters in academic gowns might be seen playing croquet. In the centre is a war memorial with a chapel on the far side and beyond some iron gates a cricket field, rugby pitch and, in those days, an enclosed rifle range.

I was shown into a panelled office, offered a chair alone at a desk with some papers on it and handed a fountain pen, with the instruction to do my best. Then whoever that person was shut the door behind him and I tried to work out how to write with this weird implement.

Back at Staples Road my friends were keen to know where I'd been the afternoon I'd left early. I was under instructions not to tell anyone but since they'd asked I bragged about this entrance exam I'd had to sit, calling it 'a kind of ten-plus' as we all knew we'd have to sit the eleven-plus in our final year. Later that day Mr Wheatley, the rumpled, grey-haired headmaster who loved football, came to find me. I was pleased to see him and I imagined that we would now have a special bond as I was the shining light of his school and he must love me.

He was furious.

He told me he'd heard about my boasting, and that he wasn't surprised since he knew what I was like, and that I'd been told not to tell anyone at Staples Road and, as a matter of fact, I hadn't done very well in the test so I should think twice before mentioning it again, which I had better not by the way.

I felt lost, I didn't care about this revelation concerning the test (how did he know how I'd done?), I didn't care if I'd got all the questions wrong, but I couldn't bear to upset Mr Wheatley. I wanted them all to be proud of me, the way they had been when we had an athletics meeting with Chigwell School and they'd put me into a one-on-one race with their star sprinter and I'd beaten him. After some conversation Chigwell School insisted the race was run again but that we should swap lanes. The other boy won and they satisfied themselves that the lane markings were wrong. Nonetheless, the boy from little Staples Road had given the visiting team the biggest cheer of the day, and everyone was proud of me and I was happy.

I was hoping that to be put forward for Bancroft's early was a similar thing, an achievement, that the teachers and my classmates would again be proud of me, but it seemed there was more to it, conversations I was not party to, and I felt I was missing something.

Soon after that Mr Wheatley came in to our classroom to tell the class who their teacher would be the following year. I knew by then that I would be at Bancroft's, though still no one had asked me if I'd rather stay.

Unexpectedly, he said that since the class was doing so well with Mrs Thorogood, she was going to move up with them into their final year. Everyone cheered. I tried to join in but I was leaving and I wouldn't be with Mrs Thorogood and I wouldn't be in the school football team and I wouldn't be Brainbox any more and I wouldn't be with my classmates that I'd known for years and I turned to face the wall and clenched against tears. I didn't look round, I didn't plead with Mr Wheatley to let me stay, or tell Mrs Thorogood that I loved her and that I wanted to stay at Staples Road for ever.

On my first day at Bancroft's, with my over-sized suit, age-six Y-fronts and brown briefcase chosen by my father to match his, I took my place in 3N. We were first years but we were called thirds. It was something to do with prep schools, as was the second year being called Remove. The N was for North House, which had the distinction of the bleakest, coldest locker room in the place. Our form tutor read the register. The first name called was Alan so I said: 'Yes.'

Simultaneously another boy also answered. I looked around for this other Alan, to find everyone looking at me. The teacher said he was asking for surnames, was I Allan? I said I was Davies, and so I remained until I skulked out of the school after the lower sixth, contemplating arson.

When I knew I was going to leave, having turned sixteen in March 1982, I shoved something into one of the plug sockets and unintentionally fused the entire sixth-form common room, causing the music to stop and silence to descend. Someone said: 'Well done, Al.' I picked up a fire extinguisher and sprayed everyone in range. One of the girls who had joined the school in sixth form tried to hide behind a curtain when everyone else scattered. Her top half was hidden but I soaked her pencil skirt and her bare legs. Even as I was doing it I knew it was not funny, just some opportunistic combination of flirting and bullying.

The school punk rocker was also leaving and he threw some very loud bangers out of the first-floor window. Like all the best anarchists, he'd evidently made plans in advance. There were consequences for that act. The disciplinarian second master was determined to get to the bottom of it. He called us individually into his office as prime suspects but found he no longer had anything to threaten us with. I sneered at him as if I'd won. I was dropping out of school to a temporary job at Doug Smith's Greengrocers on Loughton High Road, before joining four million other unemployed people in the depths of Margaret Thatcher's orchestrated recession with only a handful of O levels to my name. What a victory.

I used to be very scared of the second master. He was the Little White Bully you'd be sent to if you were in trouble. There was no one you were sent to see if you were *having* trouble; no welfare officer or school counsellor existed. At that school a boy could not have a problem, there was no protocol for that; a boy could only *be* a problem.

My older brother hated my joining him at Bancroft's a year early. Having me two years below him at Staples Road had been close enough, but one year between us for all of secondary school was an intolerable prospect. At the bus stop after my first day in September 1976, his friends asked me if I was his brother. When I said 'yes' he sent me to the back of the queue. His fellow Removes believed me but he maintained that we were not related, to such an extent that I didn't know if I should walk back to our house with him when we got off the bus.

One day, after four or five years of this behaviour, we found ourselves on the school hockey field together. We squared up with sticks in our hands and I jabbed him in the stomach with mine. By this time I was itching for the confrontation. Normally if a fight was brewing a crowd would gather but none of the other boys cared about these two snarling brothers who had lost their mummy and we were left alone. He walked away muttering his usual mantra about my stupidity.

Many years before, I'd shouted at my dad, through tears, that I knew he'd never wanted me, that he already had a boy when I was born and he'd wanted a girl. He said that wasn't true, that they had wanted another boy, to play with my brother. In saying 'they', he'd told me that Mum had also seen me as a companion for their existing son. There's little evidence of how she felt, though I do have a postcard written by her from a family holiday in the sixties. She wrote that 'the boys' liked going down to the harbour to look at the boats. To her we were a pair, so how sad that moment on the hockey field must have appeared from above, as she looked down on us squaring up and then going our separate ways. It was the only contact her two sons had at school, where they gave up on friendship and with it the chance to recall their past or share their future.

When I left Staples Road, Mrs Thorogood told me I could always come back and see everyone. After a few weeks at Bancroft's I went to visit. As I walked up to the school I looked over at the ditch that Mum had reversed her car into a few years before. There was a new kerbstone there.

I walked along the main corridor to the familiar classroom door, knocked and went in. My old class and Mrs Thorogood all looked at me. I realised I was the only one smiling. It occurred to me I should have said I was coming if I wanted a welcoming committee.

Mrs Thorogood said it was lovely to see me and I sat down near to some of the kids I used to know. Immediately, I slipped in to the kind of unappealing bragging I adopted when trying to make people like me. I whispered to them about my geography teacher at Bancroft's who threw a board rubber across the room on to the desk of two boys who were talking, showering them in chalk dust, and who had also thrown his keys at me. I presented this as a thrilling glimpse of the life awaiting them when they reached my level of maturity. They looked horrified then bored.

Shortly afterwards the school day finished and they all stood up to go home. One kid I used to know came over, I smiled and he told me that my friend Luke, who wasn't there, had said that he'd never liked me. It was as if I'd turned up to report that I didn't miss them and so they reciprocated. If only they had known that, beneath my bravado, I had on the same little pants I had worn in this classroom every day. I was still a year away from the age-appropriate paisley Y-fronts, with waistbands of purple or brown, that followed my medical exam.

Mrs Thorogood asked how Bancroft's was, and I gave the impression that it was great. She said she was pleased but looked a little pained at my lying. Had she still been my teacher it might have been appropriate for her to put her arm around me, as she had done twelve months previously when she kept me behind as the other children went to assembly. If she had, I might have burst into tears all over again.

We said goodbye and I never went back.

Beds

I walk around the big old double bed that Mum and Dad used to share, checking both sides and the bottom, to make sure the sheets and blankets are tucked in, and that the white bedspread is folded back to halfway down, its fringe just brushing the dark blue carpet. I cross to the bay window overlooking our road and arrange the pale blue flecked silk curtains so no light comes in from the street lamps. The wardrobe doors are closed and the drawers are all shut in the big chest, so now I can climb into bed.

I flatten down the sheets and blankets across my front so it looks as though no one has disturbed them, and lie as flat as possible, with my feet turned all the way outwards, imagining the bed looks empty. I keep my nose away from the sheet as I don't like Dad's smell. Once I went right down to the bottom of the bed but it was musty with a strong toe odour (a toedour), so I didn't stay down there long. In my own bed I sometimes pluck up the courage to play at the bottom, further than my feet can reach.

Dad is downstairs, eating his supper and watching the *Nine O'Clock News*. It's probably about strikes, which he hates, or the troubles in Belfast (not HMS *Belfast*, which

he loves). I listen for cars, waiting for the white beams of
their headlights to shine between the top of the curtains
and the ceiling. Each car that goes by makes the same
sound on approach and I know from the engine noise
exactly when the light will appear, in the same satisfying
arc every time.

There are Rich Tea crumbs under the covers, and on
the bedside cupboard a paperback by Alistair MacLean,
set during the war. I might have a biscuit in a minute if I
don't fall asl—

Dad kept a tin of biscuits under his bed. He used to eat
them while reading piles of paperback novels about World
War Two, escapist adventure stories that could probably
have been understood by the biscuit-loving child he was
in wartime. It was as if, in his tastes and interests, he was
mentally stuck in the war, but then it was his childhood.
He turned six a few days before it began and twelve shortly
after it ended.

If traumatic events can stunt the emotional development
of a child at the age they are when they happen, then
perhaps all children of my father's generation were left
with a comic-book view of the horror of the war, living as
they did in a post-imperial, Churchill-worshipping, heavily
propagandised Home Front reality, with intensive state
brainwashing through newspapers and radio broadcasts,
and Government-issue wool pulled over their patriotic eyes,
all of this sustaining in them a deep and lasting mistrust of
anything foreign.

Dad talked often about the war and his hatred of the
Germans, but like everyone else I knew, he never mentioned the Eastern Front or the Holocaust. I liked to climb
into his bed on a Saturday morning so he could read aloud

from my newly delivered *Valiant* in which Jerries (Germans) said '*Achtung!*' and '*Schnell*' and '*Donner und Blitzen*', and Japs (never The Japanese) shouted, '*Banzai!*'

By the time he'd bitten into the first biscuit of the night and simultaneously begun to devour tales of British heroism, Dad would have already taken me to my own bed. Perhaps I crept into their bed when Mum was alive. Did she wake to find a ragdoll me, arms splayed, mouth open, snoozing contentedly next to her, my fingers entwined in her curly black hair? Would they have allowed that?

On the left of the bed was a cupboard and on the right a rectangular stool that curved upwards at each end with a cushion on top that matched the curtains. It's safe to assume that Mum made the window dressings and then covered a piece of foam in the same fabric. She also wrapped a house brick in a piece of leftover dress material to use as a doorstop.

On top of the blue stool cushion was a paperback with a thick orange spine, a copy of Margaret Mitchell's *Gone with the Wind*. Dad sometimes mentioned that this was Mum's favourite book. It lay there unread, in memory of her. Underneath the cushion Dad concealed a sex education book. It appeared to be an illicit thing, to be consulted in situ, and not to be carried about the house. It lived there for years beneath *Gone with the Wind*, which I assumed to be a boring book for ladies given that Dad evidently hadn't read it, and I lifted that cushion time and again to look at photographs of penises and diagrams of ovaries, with the understanding that I should never speak of them.

Forty years later, thinking of my mum, I bought a copy of *Gone with the Wind* and was enthralled. The novel details the onset and the catastrophic consequences of the

American Civil War. The recruitment of men, the women left behind, the distant conflict coming ever nearer, the fear, the reality, the bloody wounds, the dead and dying, then the thieving, the collapse of slavery, the lynchings, the Ku Klux Klan, the carpet baggers, and the destruction of homesteads, families and society itself, across great swathes of the fallen Confederacy, scorched and torched by the burgeoning United States. There is a self-serving parasitic anti-hero and an embittered anti-heroine reared in the blissful white prosperity of the antebellum South and left struggling to survive amid the carnage.

It's a Pulitzer prize-winning masterpiece of historical fiction, and to think that it was lying there all those nights and I never once clamped my dad's bedside torch between my teeth and took it under the covers to read. To think my mother loved that book and I will never talk to her about it. What did she make of Scarlett O'Hara? What a frightening, frightened, devilish survivalist, of unreal beauty and staunch self-interest. Did you like her, Mum? It's true she was spirited, cunning and resourceful, but I very much doubt she could have become a Queen's Guide like you, and she would have made a terrible Akela for the 15th Chingford Cub pack.

My boyhood interest lay in the contents of the small bedside cupboard on the opposite side from the stool with the blue cushion. Inside there were copies of *Reader's Digest* and a couple of little felt-tip drawings I had done for my dad, when I was about ten, on which I had written the mysterious phrase:

I love you well enough to
know that you love me.

It seemed to make sense at the time, after Mum had died, that I loved him and he loved me. But I remember struggling to sum up my feelings, and looking back what I wrote was painfully unsure, as if I was saying: 'I know you love me. Even though you don't say it. If I feel love for *you* that means you feel it for *me* too, doesn't it?'

There was a period, perhaps around the time of the first special cuddle, when my dad and I had a kissing ritual before my bedtime. I would kiss him on his right cheek, then the nose and then twice in quick succession on the left cheek, and he would do the same to me. I needed to complete this ceremony before I could go upstairs. Granny Price saw us doing it one evening and muttered that we were 'like a couple of film stars' before turning away, which I could tell hurt both our feelings.

I wondered if, with Mum gone, these were the only kisses either Dad or I received. I'd begun to assume he lived a lonely life and was starved of affection. It didn't occur to me to think what my life was like, or what I might be missing.

Once I was in Dad's bed with everything in its place, I could reach into the bedside cupboard and pull out the thing that really interested me, his men's magazines. These were not copies of *Autocar*, which was kept under the television (with the *Radio Times* and the *TV Times* in their binder), but four or five copies of *Men Only* and *Mayfair*, laden with naked or partially clothed young women. I pored over this treasure trove and became a self-taught objectifier of the female form.

The cupboard held a hardcore magazine too, in a wrinkled brown paper bag such as a greengrocer might put sprouts in. This one had a couple of cocks in it, not just breasts and bush, in a disturbing photo-spread featuring a young couple having a threesome with a repellent old man, who presumably represented the reader. None of them were smiling, either for the camera or for each other. How did these people find themselves there? I hope the money was good, as compensation for such chronic indignity.

When I was a little older I'd take the magazines into my room, believing Dad had no idea what I was up to, but when I smuggled the brown paper bag out, it found its way back into his cupboard from my drawer. Now I knew he knew I was looking at them.

I recently searched for old copies of *Men Only* and *Mayfair* online and recognised some of the issues from my dad's collection, dated 1975. The same feeling of secretive guilt returned when I ordered them. On their arrival I was immediately familiar with the thick, glossy pages, much superior to those in my own magazines back then, *Look-in* and *Look and Learn*. I found that I recognised all of the girls instantly, after forty years, and wondered what became of Madeline and Elspeth and especially Meg. They'd all be the other side of the menopause by now.

I'd forgotten the little articles that ran with each pictorial. Madeline, it seems, was initially reluctant to undress. The *Men Only* writer had a theory: 'Perhaps the problem was all the bustle and the activity which confused and frightened her ... some tears were shed and some time spent talking it all over. Slowly she relaxed.'

Well done, lads; that one nearly got away. Familiar as I was with an older man cajoling you out of your clothes before objectifying your nudity in a thoroughly impersonal way, it did not occur to me that the same thing had happened to these girls, who were not much older than me.

Now I see Madeline, in her yellow thigh-length woollen tights and white platform sandals, in a new (surprisingly natural) light.

Men Only women were sometimes canvassed on their view of the world, though it was implicitly amusing that you would ask them at all, never mind care for their answers. Meg appears to have tailored her ideas specifically for a readership that had come for submissive sex objects: 'I suppose careers are fine for some women, but I'm not one of them,' she said, to which *Men Only* added: 'She's a girl who clearly enjoys living with her lovely head in the clouds.'

And there she is, wearing over-the-knee tights emphasising her thighs, with very little make-up, no fake tan or tattoos, her fingers coyly in her knickers and a bit of old radiator in the back of shot.

All these familiar women without underwear, that I shouldn't have been looking at when I was pre-pubescent, from the top-shelf magazines high up above *Valiant*, are mixed in with the memory of my dad sneaking around from room to room. In buying these magazines and leaving them out for me to find, Dad succeeded in persuading me that he wanted pictures of Martie, 'a lot of men think I want just sex,' or Elspeth, 'the first impression you get . . . is of a giggling light-hearted well-shaped teenager', when actually any younger brothers they had would be more up his street.

In many of the pictures the subject has her eyes tightly closed or is looking away from the photographer, perhaps in an effort to shut out the sordid compliments and the smell of cigarettes. Looking at Elspeth now, flat on her back, eyes shut, I realise she looks ready to be lifted on to a mortuary slab for autopsy. All of the girls are lounging around meekly, as if recovering from a general anaesthetic that caused their clothes to fall off. Perhaps a young female corpse is a common male fantasy. Pulse and regular breathing are optional. It's possible that, for a girl like Elspeth, sex with a *Men Only* reader may have had the erotic appeal of a coroner's inspection.

But you knew what you were buying; an interview with Billy Connolly, Fiona Richmond on a yacht, readers' letters, all a bit smutty with a thin veneer of faux-elegance.

Putting those magazines in such an accessible place, knowing that his young son had found them, might be considered a lure. Commonly, child molesters are introducing the idea of nudity and touching to their victims.

One night as I lay on my bedroom floor, pyjama bottoms round my ankles, masturbating quietly while gazing at beautiful Joanie in *Mayfair*, my dad walked in. I rolled on to my front and shoved the magazine under the bed, thinking he'd leave when he realised I was ... undressed. But in breaching the privacy of my bedroom time and again over the years he'd established that my naked body was his to enjoy, so he stood there, on the other side of my bed, grinning.

'What are you doing?' he said.

'Nothing,' I said.

He chuckled. 'What are you *doing*?'

'*Nothing.*' (*Go away, I hate your stupid haircut, your smooth, featureless torso, the way your pelvis hangs forward, your long thighs with the gap in between, your arms hanging slightly behind you, the side-parting, exactly as your mummy combed it when you were a boy, the smug power game, your poor taste in books, the way you serve at tennis, the way you put your knife and fork down on your plate and then masticate like a llama while you never, ever, under any circumstances, think of anything*

*interesting, diverting or amusing to say, nothing to say at all, in
fact, that isn't related to sport on the television, which is never
off so none of us learn how to have a conversation, I hate the
stains in your underpants, and now you have caught me wanking and you won't leave, so what's in it for you? Do you want to
watch? What if I roll over and ask you to 'please, Daddy, stay
until I come and then tuck me in'? Is that what you want, you
unspeakable creep, you child molesting pervert? I can't wait to
never have to see you again, go away.)*

I couldn't get my pyjamas back up round my waist. I was
lying face down, showing a white moon in the gloom. He
peered over the bed, still grinning, while I tried to prevent
a glimpse of my erection, which he seemed keen to see.
Unless he just liked me powerless and vulnerable.

It was humiliating but if I wanted to keep my cock
hidden, and I believed it to be malformed after the doctor's
remarks at my school medical, then I'd have to wait it out.
He tried to persuade me to stand up but if I was noisily
unwilling he'd have to relent, which he eventually did.

What were his thoughts after he turned away and went
back to his room? Was he angry or frustrated? Did he loathe
me, or himself?

Nothing comes to my mind when I imagine the work-
ings of his.

I know *now* that he was sexually interested in all boys
of my age, but he couldn't advance his grooming of me
because I was unwilling and my sister was a few feet away
in the next room. He'd done some cuddling, some nude
manipulation, introduced girlie magazines and now managed to interrupt me wanking. Was this the dream scenario?
He seemed happy to have caught me at it. But what if I had
asked him to join me on the bed for a next-level special

cuddle and then reached for *his* cock? Would he have allowed that? Would we have embarked on a silent movie of homosexual incest, with full-screen dialogue cards:

Will my penis feel the same as yours one day, Daddy?

Or:

Now let us compare genitals, Father.

Or would he have recoiled, unable to go through with his fantasy made real? A sexually curious teenage boy, willing to nustle up and nestle in, to canoodle and caress, to squeeze and pump and bite, to experiment, to go on all fours on the nylon-mix sheets. Or does Daddy only like photos of those things, and only of all boys together?

Or perhaps he did just want to watch me?

He was vague about the whole thing, giving off all sorts of mixed signals. It seems a bit much, in hindsight, for him to have expected me to make all the right moves in our fledgling sexual relationship. I was eager to please him, of course, but how could I do that when it all felt so awkward and embarrassing?

I remained a hospitable, self-sacrificing partner in my later adult sexual relationships, Dad's haunting legacy perhaps, and I never became any more able to shake off the idea that finding out what the other person wants is a silent guessing game in the dark. Nor did I realise that a large part of what they all wanted was something my father never considered: my happiness.

It never occurred to me to call his bluff. I had no interest. Perhaps all groomers, abusers and molesters, even rapists, secretly hope or believe that there is a degree of reciprocation, that the victim wants this to happen, or that they will come round to the idea in time. But this is emphatically not the case. However compliant their behaviour, however frequently the abused appear to invite further abuse else-where, it's because they have been damaged. The only thing that really grows is revulsion, and it lasts a lifetime.

Sometimes I recall a pleasant memory of my dad in my bedroom. I'm in my bed and he's coming in to say good-night. On the floor next to me I have an Action Man army field tent complete with a fold-out map table, a chair, a camp bed and a jeep parked outside. I have very neatly put my best Action Man to bed. He's in his tent under some covers, realistic hair on the realistic pillow (and eyes wide open but we can ignore that). My dad thought this endear-ing. He liked the way I'd set up the camp next to the head of my bed, just behind the door, as if I had a little friend who was going to be alongside me as I slept.

Of course I'd been all round both my room and Action Man's tent to ensure that everything was in its rightful place, allowing me to attempt sleep. I played with that Action Man for years, until one day, as an older boy, I pinned him to my brother's dartboard and then threw darts at him as hard as I could. They kept bouncing off him, none would stick, I'd miss him more often than not, and if I did score a hit the dart would get snagged in his battered uniform at best.

In frustration I took him down from the dartboard, exposed his chest, and pushed a dart through the hard plastic into his hollow interior. He looked at me with the same eyes. I pulled out the dart and there was a dark hole in him, though once he was dressed you'd never know.

Housekeepers

Some time after Mum died, Dad searched for a surrogate to look after his children, and to undertake all domestic duties. His own mother and mother-in-law could only fill the breach up to a point. So he sought out a live-in house-keeper by placing a small ad in *The Lady*.

The ad was a success. An applicant was selected. She arrived, disappeared into the box room at the top of the stairs where she was to sleep, and hardly ever came out. If she did appear, it was not to strike up a conversation. This conduct wasn't what Dad had in mind for the role, which was most likely a combination of Julie Andrews in *The Sound of Music* and Julie Andrews in *Mary Poppins*. But our version was probably depressed. So she was, in modern parlance, 'let go'.

Undeterred, Dad tried again with more success, and employed a younger housekeeper who was chatty and like-able, I used to enjoy being picked up from primary school in her red Austin 1100. She had a traumatic first day with us because I was hit by a car on Station Road, while cycling with my brother to Cubs at St Mary's Church Hall. I had turned right to cross the road, without looking, heading for the pavement on the other side. I remember my brother shouting my name and then there was an impact and I was lying in front of a Cortina. I was most worried about my bike, which had skidded several yards up the street. The driver helped me up and sat me in the back of his car. There was an old man in there I took to be his father: 'That was a stupid thing to do, wasn't it?' he said. I concurred and we waited in silence. I presumed he meant that I was stupid, but looking back he might have considered a stiff word with his son, who'd managed to hit a slow-moving nine-year-old cyclist, clearly visible in front of him, on a wide road with no other traffic.

Thrillingly, I was brought home in the front of a police van with a bandage round my leg. I had hoped to have a cast but no such luck. The new housekeeper seemed agitated by the incident as if it had happened to her and kept saying:

'On my first day!'

Other than that I remember she liked watching Wimbledon on TV, and she stripped to her bra to wash her hair in the kitchen sink, which Mum definitely did not do. She was there in 1975, I know this because Arthur Ashe won the Men's Singles title against Jimmy Connors and I went back and forth to the kitchen to keep her up to speed with the score.

Either before or after her, it's hard to remember, came Emma.

We never asked any questions of these women; who they were, where they came from, how they came to be living with us, whether they had children of their own. Polite curiosity and personal interest were among the unlearned skills of my childhood. Emma was the only one I asked about her age. She was thirty-three, quite tall, with curly blonde hair.

Emma always took a moment at the end of the day to

suggest something for me to dream about at night. It was our special little routine. I'd say goodnight to my dad as he ate his supper, prepared by Emma, in front of the TV. Then I'd go to her in the kitchen and she'd give me something to think of before I went to sleep. She seemed to enjoy coming up with a new one each day. One evening we were sat together at the bottom of the stairs, me in my pyjamas, when Dad came out of the dining room. The look of tired irritation across his face signified trouble. I was not supposed to be up. I tried for pre-emptive defence, saying I just wanted something to dream about, but it was futile. He told her, in that terse, impatient voice, that I should be in *bed* and turned his back, before she could reply, satisfied he'd broken up the party. When Emma disappeared from my life soon afterwards, with no goodbye, it only confirmed what I'd long suspected, that Dad wanted rid of people who made him angry, and no one made him angrier than me.

To my shame, the lasting memory I have of Emma is of watching her through the keyhole when she was in the bath. The taps were at the far end of the little room so my eye was blinking away behind her. When she unexpectedly stood up and faced the door I held my breath in case I gave myself away; I can still see her clearly enough that if I were an artist I could paint her, though perhaps only with a keyhole surround. She was facing me, standing in soapy foam, long-limbed with square shoulders, looking down as she rinsed patches of white bubbles from her flat torso. I stared at her round breasts with their dark nipples and at her pubic hair, darker than her blonde curls. Looking back, I wonder what sort of a boy I was becoming, already abused by that point and now a voyeur. She was oblivious to the act of espionage going on a few feet away. It never happened again because, no sooner had I fallen in love with Emma, than she was gone.

Dad gave up on the housekeepers for a while. Perhaps my sister was now at school and old enough to dress herself in the mornings and I was soon to be yanked away from Mrs Thorogood and sent on the bus to Bancroft's, so maybe he felt he didn't need to have a woman in the house full time. My brother and I were struggling to share a room happily so he went back to the box room, and I had the back bedroom to myself.

Dad now hired 'tea ladies', who just came in the afternoon. The best of those was Jenny. She had a partly affectionate, partly amused nature, with a light hand on the tiller of inter-sibling navigation. My sister and I were especially fond of her. I wished she would live with us but she had a husband at home. For a while in 1976 I was being taught at school by Mrs Thorogood, taught the piano by Mr Clutterbuck, and having my tea cooked by Jenny. Furthermore, my first special cuddle from Dad appeared to be a one-off and was receding into the past. He took me to Lord's and The Oval to watch Test Cricket, which I still love to do, and I began to thrive at Staples Road, rising from mediocrity to the top of the class as if I'd experienced a quantum leap.

But then Jenny took another job elsewhere, Mr Clutterbuck died, and I was sent to Bancroft's a year early. Dad tried another housekeeper for a while. My brother was forced to come back and share a bedroom with me, which was when relations became so bad that Dad had the partition erected.

The lady who was to be our last housekeeper wandered into the living room on her first day, saw me and said:

'Somebody's sitting too close to the television.' I decided I didn't like her on the spot. I'd remembered her coming to the house to be interviewed. She was older than the young housekeepers, and not a bit like Emma. I couldn't believe Dad had chosen her.

One day, towards the end of my second year at Bancroft's, I came home to find that she was not there. In my bedroom there was an envelope with my name on it. It was a letter from her:

When you read this I shall have left. I do not like saying goodbye, so that is the reason I said nothing this morning. You will always have a special place in my affections Alan, so take care of yourself.
My warmest regards to your brother and sister and your father.
My loving regards to you.

This was a surprise, and I was pleased that someone had finally noticed how much nicer I was than everyone else, though I was disappointed that she also sent her regards to them, which I did not pass on. It was so abnormal for me to receive praise that I attributed it to her being a bit of an oddball. Of course she went away; in my life all the nicest people had done that. I still have the letter. It's dated 26 June 1978 and is therefore one of the few concrete clues as to the chronology of events.

Soon after that my brother returned to his old box room, and the paper-thin partition in the back bedroom was taken down, meaning I had it all to myself. And soon Dad began to visit, now I was twelve and then thirteen, while my brother and sister were asleep in their own rooms.

On the plus side, no housekeeper meant we would now have a tea lady again and to our delight Jenny returned.

She was exactly as I remembered her. The only new thing I now noticed was that she always left her handbag on the red swirly carpet in the hall. I couldn't tell you where she left her handbag during her first stint with us, but I wasn't the same boy by this time.

The bag was always in the same place, across from the telephone shelf and close to the front door, conveniently out of sight from the kitchen or living room. I could not resist the temptation and helped myself, pilfering pound notes, or fives, or even a ten whenever I could. Jenny never said anything, though she must have noticed. This went on for some time and enabled me to buy all sorts of odd items that I could smuggle home and hide. I was only buying them so I could keep them in secret. I couldn't let anyone see what I'd bought since no one could know about my riches.

I was accumulating odd things, such as books of railway locomotive numbers, as used by trainspotters, even though I had no interest in trains or spotting, I just liked the covers. I kept all my comics, some that Dad had delivered for me each week with the newspaper but also dozens of American Marvel comics he wouldn't recognise. I bought scores of Panini football stickers, going out of my way each day to the only newsagent that sold them, and I hoarded the lot, every toy and souvenir, sticker and comic, I never swapped or threw anything away.

Then one day my dad told me he'd been looking through my drawers for some library books he needed to take back. I suspect he was actually looking for his porn mags that I'd 'borrowed'. He'd come across all kinds of stuff I'd either shoplifted or bought with money pinched from Jenny's handbag. It must have looked strange to him, like uncovering a secret life.

He knew I was capable of theft, and of bizarre behaviour. On one occasion he received a free pair of pocket binoculars with a magazine. I secreted them away, then wrapped them in brown paper and put the package among the presents that were hidden under his bed for my birthday. The following morning, after I'd opened everything he'd bought for me, I said that I thought there was another present, he said that there wasn't, and then he and my brother and sister watched speechless as I went under his bed and 'found' the last 'present'. I opened it up to reveal the missing binoculars. Dad remarked that they looked very similar to the ones that had been delivered to him. I said that Granny Price must have bought them for me, and I kept them, just like that, stolen from my own father brazenly in plain sight.

But this new stash he'd found was extraordinary and he had questions.

'Why do you need a stopwatch?'

'I just wanted one.'

'I'd have bought you one.'

HAHAHAHAHAHAHA. No you wouldn't.

Part of the reason I did what I did was because Dad didn't like to spend, whereas I did like to spend but had no money.

Desperately thinking on my feet I invented a source for some of the stuff, a boy called Coote at Bancroft's. Dad didn't know Coote so it felt like a safe lie, for about five seconds, then he said we'd need to thank this boy's father. Of course Coote was nothing to do with it, I barely knew him. He had the look of a trainspotter, with his glasses held together with a plaster, but he was more the maverick intellectual and not in the under-achieving peer group I was part of, now my primary school Brainbox days were behind me. It felt as though Dad was going to pick up the phone book any second, and there might be only one Coote in there. I couldn't allow that call to happen.

Masonry was falling from the edifice of my constructed life (theft, accumulation, solitude), I had to do something or the lot could come down, so I blurted out that I'd stolen some money, hoping for mercy.

'How much?' he said.

'Twenty-five pounds,' I lied.

Although that was a sizeable sum for a twelve-year-old, the real amount was far more than that. I burst into tears of relief as I unburdened my conscience. Dad adopted the tone of a caring parent, but what he actually said found an extra notch on the rack I'd roped myself to.

He told me, in a gentle 'there, there, don't cry' voice, that Jenny's husband had left her because of the missing money. He knew that I had no way of verifying that or even really understanding what it meant, but he also knew that I loved Jenny and that I would feel terrible about what I'd done.

I can't fully remember the order of everything, the thefts, the confession, when Jenny left us, or when I was told that her husband had left her because of me. I think she'd already gone when Dad told me that, or else I might have asked her about it. It's all so distant, only the most impactful emotional memories remain. One of those is the day Jenny told us that she was leaving, when she seemed even more upset than we were. But after the tears she was gone, like Emma, like Mum.

Each loss was connected to the last as if with a thick knotted rope tied to somewhere deep inside. The rope is always there, ready to have a new length tied on, to be grabbed by the next life event, so if pain is felt it is connected to the pain right down at the beginning of the rope. This might compound the feelings sometimes, but often the familiarity of the emotion, of the rope tightening, means that it does not cause you to fall down, it is just more of the same, almost expected, and doesn't necessarily cause great waves of shock and hurt.

I've learned that children who suffer sexual abuse may develop symptoms of Obsessive Compulsive Disorder, and hoarding is one of those. The hanging on to items, the inability to quantify the value of evidently worthless things (broken toys, old comics), an excessive emotional attachment to objects, all represent an attempt to focus on something tangible, a self-created diversion from a hidden emotional crisis, usually at home. So hoarding becomes important, as does the accumulation of items that have no actual use to the hoarder, and likely won't be looked at again. They are gathered up and added to the growing stash that provides faux emotional support by virtue of being under the hoarder's control. This lingers on. I still have boxes of useless stuff piled in a room up one flight of stairs from where I'm writing.

A few years ago I had the opportunity to have an exchange of emails with Jenny's son. I was grateful for the chance to ask about his parents' divorce all those years ago. He said that nothing about my stealing from her had ever been mentioned. I'd evidently caught him by surprise. It was as if he didn't really understand the question. I told him how fond I was of his mother and it seemed she'd spoken equally fondly of her time with us.

Maybe Dad meant what he said, believing that a husband would inevitably leave a wife who appeared to be keeping money from him.

I don't know how much I took, maybe sixty pounds, or eighty. I don't know if Dad gave back the twenty-five pounds I'd confessed to stealing. At the time he convinced me that I'd ruined Jenny's life, and that I was the author of my own and my sister's unhappiness, while casting a shadow of shame across him he'd have to live with for ever. With hindsight, it might seem a lot of fuss, until you tap the numbers into an online inflation calculator and discover that eighty quid in the late seventies is the equivalent of around five hundred pounds today.

Coins

The first part of the school year at Bancroft's is referred to as the Michaelmas Term, just as it is at another venerable institution the school may have deemed its equal, such was its opinion of itself, namely The Royal Courts of Justice.

Michaelmas is a minor Christian Festival named for the Archangel Michael who battled Satan in heaven, which led to fallen angels being thrown down to Earth. Michael (who was so impressive some people suspect he might have been Jesus) also gives his name to some daisies, and a range of underwear at Marks & Spencer. Any angels who fell into my school during Michaelmas may have thought the lack of heating in the History block punishment enough for their misdemeanours before God.

Colder even than the classrooms were the school's Snakes Lane playing fields, where we would walk every Wednesday in Michaelmas to endure rugby, after which some of us would take the tube home. It's only two stops from Woodford to Loughton. Close to the station was a newsagent with a wall of newspapers, comics and out-of-reach dirty magazines. By now I was shoplifting to order for other people in my year. I went in to take a magazine for a well-spoken boy who would never dream of stealing anything, and who would then buy it from me at a huge discount. He and a few others spread out across the wide pavement outside, bags strewn around, baiting each other out of boredom, and peering through the shop window every now and then in the hope I'd be getting on with it so they could go home for tea. With hindsight they were only drawing attention to the whole operation.

The method I planned to deploy was to conceal the target publication inside a copy of *Whizzer and Chips* and then buy that. I'd done it before but symptoms of anxiety surfaced immediately. My hands began to shudder and my heart threw itself around inside my chest, making it hard for air to reach my lungs, which had flattened themselves against the back of my ribcage. A deadening weakness filled my legs as a warning that, should I need to run, I would flop along with knees like water-filled balloons. I drifted towards the shelves of magazines as if on a lunar walk, avoiding eye contact, close to multiple organ failure.

I also conformed, unwittingly, to a late-seventies identikit for a shoplifter: a teenage boy in school uniform with an Adidas holdall. The tangible rewards on offer didn't outweigh the risk. I'd only receive a few coins for the magazine. But there was also the imagined confirmation of my status as the Upper Fourth's top thief, despite being its youngest member at thirteen. I scanned the shelves for the expensive glossy periodical on order.

On these missions I convinced myself I was showing a daring that was beyond my older peers, while failing to recognise that they were using me. Always carefully less impressed than I'd expected, they withheld the praise I craved, so I stole more and more, hoping for respect, but they gave me puzzled, bored glances and shared muttered remarks that I couldn't make out, suggesting they thought me reckless, or was it stupid, or stupidly reckless? I felt on the outside of a group, which was a habitual state of mind I unconsciously brought with me from home and established in my school life. The patterns of these new relationships carried such familiarity that the risk-taking was almost a comfort, which is why I could do it, and became the reason I made the type of mistakes I did.

Unlike at primary school, I was unable to shine at Bancroft's, either in the classroom or in the playground. I couldn't bridge the gap that being younger opened up. I felt the need to effect some change in the perception of me, to move myself inwards. But was I even on the outside? Only my own actions set me apart, otherwise I was middle-ranking, but I could see no salvation in working hard at school when I'd never be top of the class. So convinced was I of my worthlessness among my peers, I took extreme measures to appeal to them but only managed to cast myself out, a poor man's fallen angel.

As I went up to the counter with a thickened copy of *Whizzer and Chips* the manager moved the shop assistant aside, and immediately I knew he'd been watching me. He was my worst kind of authority figure, a grave middle-aged man, possibly a father himself. My mind buckled like a sus-pension bridge in high winds. Individual thoughts dropped into the murky waters below like cars flipped over the side. I was rattled and psychologically incoherent. Any bystander would have seen it was time to drop the periodicals and flee. They might even have called out 'just leave the shop' as helpful spectators at Wimbledon yelled 'just play your game' to John McEnroe during his show-court meltdowns.

The manager took the comic from my hand. He could

see the hidden magazine. I could see his tie. The tie said he didn't work behind the till, since he'd risen to a white-collar position, but he still knew how to ring up some numbers and he did that quickly, fixing me in the middle of a transaction.

'What's this?' he said, with the second magazine slipping into view.

I said I wanted both and he pointed out that I hadn't offered enough money.

Just concentrate on your game, John! Don't let them get to you!

I should have said that I'd made a mistake and that I couldn't afford them.

There's no law against taking two magazines to a shop counter and leaving them there, John!

Instead, I panicked as he looked me straight in the face. I couldn't control my expression, couldn't harden myself, he could see me melting pathetically. How many fledgling robbers from the nearby comprehensive had he caught since the start of Michaelmas alone? Now these rugger buggers from the posh school were turning up on a Wednesday stealing copies of *Country* fucking *Life*.

It was as if he and I both knew what I was and I couldn't fool him. I then came up with such an odd solution he almost smiled, as my disconnected thoughts reached out to one another on their way out to sea. I put appeasement and escape together and offered him more money than was necessary for both items.

'Bribery as well as theft?' he said.

I may have stopped hearing properly after that, since I remember little else. I began to question my eyesight too as I could no longer see any of my peers on the pavement outside.

While I waited in a back office, he rang my school and spoke to the Lilliputian second master. The school, apart from its term names, did not otherwise resemble The Royal Courts of Justice. It was a totalitarian state tyrannised, like others historically, by a short-arse. Now this knee-high was in the chain of events it wouldn't be long before my father rushed to concur with him.

The next day after school I got off the bus carrying a letter for my dad from the tiny teacher who belonged in *The Borrowers*. Anxiety was filling me as if it were a dense liquid being poured into a wide hole in the top of my head. My lungs skulked to the back of my ribs again but I found enough breath to walk up the hill past all the front gardens, feeling vulnerable, as if everyone might soon know what I was.

I didn't mention my plight to my siblings, or anyone else, since no one I knew would say: 'Don't worry about it, everyone nicks stuff, I'd like to kick that pocket autocrat in the face.'

It was to be just Dad and me in the loop, a further secret in our unequal pact. I knew he'd turn the screw somehow but the clever card he played was unexpected. He said he was going to *have* to tell his brother, my Uncle Pat. I expected this incident to be another thing mixed into our man-and-boy dance of unmentionable acts, with me further squashed down into a cube of shame while he gloated passive-aggressively before entering my room that night in all his tallness to rub his hands over my flinching naked buttocks, the everyday consequences for a schoolboy miscreant.

But it seemed he really wanted to tell Uncle Pat, perhaps because he had noticed how much I liked Uncle Pat.

Everyone liked Uncle Pat.

'Why have you got to tell Uncle Pat?' I said.

'I *have* to.'

Uncle Pat was genial and not inclined to voice a bad opinion of anybody, but perhaps even he could be persuaded to think badly of me. We were given Sunday lunch at his house regularly, made by Auntie Carol. Mum was never mentioned at these occasions, or at any other time, but I didn't notice that, the food was hot and plentiful and I was encouraged to eat like one of Enid Blyton's Famous Five in a stranger's farmhouse kitchen. I pulled a lot of wishbones and gorged on Yorkshire Pudding, Dutch Apple Pie and Gooseberry Fool. I was also delighted to learn that Pat supported Arsenal, further confirmation of his outstanding character.

There was no reason for Dad to tell his brother about the newsagent incident, and Dad hadn't thought to make one up when I asked him why. He hated justifying his choices. It caused his cheeks to redden and his temper to shorten. He'd begin by repeating himself MORE LOUDLY.

'I *have* to.'

'Why?'

'I HAVE to.'

'But why?'

'*I HAVE TO!*'

'WHY?'

'Don't you DARE answer me back!'

If I could go back to that house now I'd take my young self by the hand, down the hall to the telephone on its shelf, and I'd dial Uncle Pat's number before handing over the receiver. Then the younger me would feel the words come to his lips even as he looked around wondering where I'd gone:

'Uncle Pat, it's Alan. Hello. I'm ringing because I've been caught trying to steal a magazine from a shop. I did it for money. Someone in my class was going to pay me for it. I never have any money to buy anything, and I like being the best thief in the year as it's some status at least. It's been a struggle for me since I was taken out of primary school where I was happy and put into that place. I know you went there too and so did your father and your son. I don't know if you all liked it there or hated it but I *have* to pretend to enjoy it. Though in truth I've been a thief for years, it started when I was primary-school age. It may have begun after my mum died and my dad started . . . looking after us on his own. I'll take anything I can get my hands on. I was once caught trying to steal a water pistol. I said it must have fallen into my bag. I've been stealing money from Jenny's handbag for ages. Jenny is our tea lady when we get in from school. Maybe you know her; I think she lives in your road, actually. If I babysit for my sister's little friends opposite I go round the house looking for coins. I do try to earn money too. As well as babysitting, I washed cars for a couple near us at the weekend but then they said they were going on holiday and I didn't need to come. I cycled past one day and they were there playing tennis. I wanted to get a paper round but Dad wouldn't let me. He only gives me £1.35 a week. He gives my brother £1.40 and my sister £1.30. They don't really need any money since they don't spend it, so I take coins from their piggy banks. Dad keeps coins in NatWest bank bags in the top drawer in his room. I take some of those sometimes. He also has notes in another drawer but I wouldn't take one of those unless there were plenty there so he might think he'd miscounted. I think about money often and spend a lot of time alone trying to get it. Dad counts every penny. He even writes it down in a cashbook when he buys a choc ice. Was he always like that with money? Was your dad like it? Come to think of it, Grandpa never slips me a few coins, though he always seems to have Fox's Glacier Mints to hand. Do you know he took me to Trafalgar Square by myself? Did he take you there when you were a boy? He always watches cricket on the telly if he comes to our house, and then falls asleep. Anyway, I won't keep you; Dad was just saying he was going to tell you about me stealing this thing that I didn't actually steal, presumably to damage my relationship with you. There are things he does at night that I'll never tell you about that might well damage *his* relationship with you. I think he'd like to keep me in a place where I'm not well thought of in case I spill the beans on him. Then he can say that I've always been a thief and a liar. And it's true, I have. Hope to see you for Sunday lunch but I expect you won't want me there now. I've never stolen anything from your house. I love coming round, playing in the garden and hearing your jokes. I'd better go because Dad is bound to get cross about the phone bill in a minute. He makes me pretty anxious, to be honest. I have very low self-esteem indeed. Goodbye.'

I found out years later that Uncle Pat disliked Dad, something best illustrated by his opposition to him joining his beloved golf club. Dad persuaded two other members to support his application and joined anyway, despite knowing his brother, who had been a member for years, didn't want him there. Dad wrote up pages of notes on all his golf rounds, filling lines and lines in tiny handwriting, detailing hundreds of shots, and his anxiety about improving and how he was perceived by the other golfers, thousands of words about his thoughts and feelings, but only about golf.

It was his other obsession during his retirement, alongside hardcore gay teen porn.

I also learned that when Carol went into decline with Alzheimer's she once stood up and left the room when Dad came in, revealing some long-concealed feeling as sufferers of that condition frequently do. I don't know why she couldn't stand him. Before they died my Uncle Pat and Auntie Carol each suffered from Alzheimer's while they were still together in their family home, only occasionally emerging from their individual fog into simultaneous recognition and lucidity. It's unbearable that their lives should have ended like that, confused and cantankerous, together but apart. I don't know if Dad actually told his brother about my shoplifting trouble all those years ago, only that Pat never mentioned it to me, and always treated me warmly.

Following the incident in the newsagent, three people now had power over me, each with their own agenda, and none of them would admit that no offence had taken place. What is it about teenage boys that makes men act so punitively?

The manager wanted to punish me for plotting to steal from his shop; doubtless he felt besieged by light-fingered boys.

The bonsai second master wanted to preserve the name of the school and strike fear into yet another boy who had the audacity to be the same height as him.

For my dad, it was a gift, further proof of my untrustworthy character, and of how difficult I made his life when things were *damn well hard enough* as a widower. The upside for him was that my worsening reputation meant no one would believe me about anything else. He acted as if behaviour like mine (boy nicks thing) was beyond his comprehension. He'd never do anything wrong, upright citizen that he was, respectable, civilised and legally parked, he was in the privileged position of having absolute power in a world where racism, misogyny and in-house child molestation lay within the parameters of acceptability. If you queued properly, had a current tax disc in your car and always watched the Queen's Speech at Christmas then you were exemplary (provided you were English).

It was agreed that I would return to the shop the following Saturday to work in the backyard clearing away rubbish. This was presented as a show of leniency, as if more serious consequences involving the police had been decided against, for which I should be grateful. The police might have pointed out that I hadn't even left the shop, and that really I needed to have crossed the threshold on to the pavement, where the manager could have executed a citizen's arrest.

You've every right to question the call, John; stand your ground!

But perhaps the manager was afraid I'd run off. I scored tries at rugby against boys older than me because I was fast, though if they caught me they screwed me up like a crisp packet.

I gave up shoplifting, which may have kept The Book Shop on Loughton High Road in business since I had been stealing from there for months, and I enjoyed clearing up the yard, it was satisfying and no one bothered me. I'd felt disappointed that I couldn't go to the Tottenham Hotspur home game my dad had tickets for. He'd pulled a sad face as he informed me that I'd miss the match, and succeeded in making me feel bad about that, too, but I didn't think about it once that afternoon. I didn't like Spurs anyway, they reminded me of him. I liked Arsenal, thanks to Mum buying me their shirt.

I remember sitting on exactly the same seat in the same tube carriage on the way back from the newsagent as I had on the way there. It was identifiable by the dried and blackened chewing gum stuck to it, which had travelled all the way to West Ruislip and back. That pleased me, but I didn't wish I had anyone to tell it to. I didn't wish to speak to anyone at all. I could clear up the yard alone, travel on the tube alone; to be alone was better than any of the alternatives.

Like a fledgling fallen angel, I bunked the fare there and back by using an old ticket and concealing the date with my thumb. I knew that, now shoplifting was over, I'd need to find a new way to get money, so that one day I wouldn't have to go home at all.

Stamps

After Jenny left the second time, we had a new tea lady. She was an unsmiling, short woman, with dark hair and an accent similar to our Spanish next-door neighbour, who used to exhaust herself yelling the place down and then sunbathe in the garden topless when her three boys were at school. The worst thing about *la nueva dama* was that she kept her *bolso de mano* in the kitchen, which made it difficult to steal from. Although I'd retired from shoplifting, or any crime that fell under the jurisdiction of outsiders, I still felt able to bring a little lawlessness into the family home, where many normal rules appeared not to apply. My old habits were not dead. Eventually, after several attempts at loitering nearby, I found myself alone in there and I quickly put my hand into her reddish leather bag, opening it up to look inside. At that moment she came in and we locked eyes and froze. It was a stand-off, maybe she was Mexican.

I had recently discovered, in the broom cupboard in the kitchen, several books of Green Shield and Co-op stamps. These were rewards given out in shops, one stamp for every sixpence spent. There were still silver sixpence pieces around for years after decimalisation. You would look for them in Christmas puddings; they were the size of a new penny, but now worth 2½p.

I had stumbled across a treasure trove. I held the books in my hand, as Mum must once have done, and made the assumption that Dad had kept them as a token, a keepsake, a remembrance.

The possibility of cloning Mum from the traces of saliva under the stamps didn't cross my mind. We didn't do DNA at Staples Road, we did bark rubbing. All I thought about was that the Co-op books were worth money.

Green Shield Stamps were bought by shops and petrol stations and distributed to customers, like Nectar points, to be redeemed for items in their catalogue. To collect Co-op stamps you needed to go to one of their stores and the one in Loughton was the Biggest Supermarket in Europe, or so we believed; it had become folklore. It may have been superseded by some enormo-store on the continent but when it opened in 1962 it was unsurpassed. Some people did wonder why the biggest shop ever built would appear in sleepy suburban Epping Forest but most enjoyed the prestige.

The Forest was also home to Loughton Camp, whose earth walls I scrambled up as a boy, and where the woman we knew as Boadicea (but now referred to as Boudica) was said to have hidden with her Iceni tribe from the Roman invaders. Boudica's husband had been an important tribal leader who established relations with the Romans. After he died Boudica's daughters were raped in front of her (like all child abuse, this went unmentioned at school). She led an uprising that destroyed London as well as the Roman capital at Colchester and the town of Verulamium, now St

Alban's, where I went on a school trip nearly two thousand years later.

Now Boudica's former home, Loughton, was at last taking the lead again. And as before, our island nation would never be the same, for this new supermarket was literally bigger than the Church.

Judging by the amount of stamps I'd found, Mum must have been there almost daily, though by law it was closed on Sundays in case it put St Mary's out of business. I find it hard to understand why I can't remember us in the shop: Mum folding sheets of stamps into her purse, my sister perched in a trolley, me looking up at them, on countless shopping trips between 1968 when we moved from Chingford, and 1972 when Mum stopped shopping altogether. It's not uncommon to remember virtually nothing before the age of six, but for me it's uncommonly frustrating.

I do remember standing among legs and skirts when Mum stopped to talk to people on the High Road. I was unable to hold her attention, and unhappy to be left out and made to wait down below out of sight, which is presumably why those moments have stayed with me.

Other things I recall just because I saw them so often: the butcher turning a handle to make mincemeat for her, the greengrocer emptying potatoes from a diamond-shaped weighing dish into an old holdall we brought for that purpose. Dried mud puffed up in a cloud of noise and dust as the spuds thundered into the dark bag and lay immediately silent as if they'd gone back underground.

Dad still collected Green Shield Stamps at petrol stations. He'd let me do the licking and sticking. I put those books back in the cupboard where they may have remained until long after Green Shield became Argos. The Co-op books, though, were a temptation. They had wide blue covers with two staples at the side and about twenty pages filled with stamps. These were ready to exchange. Why hadn't they been taken in? If Dad knew they were here wouldn't he have gone for the cash? Perhaps only the person who took the book home could redeem them. It had to be worth a try, though. It was free money.

It was difficult to do anything unnoticed in the kitchen; my brother might wander in for a Jaffa Cake at any minute. I had to make a decision quickly. I put one book up my jumper.

When I took it to the Co-op I was as nervous as a shop-lifter. I'd convinced myself that Dad didn't know about the books, and that I should have told him about them. Did you have to be a grown-up to redeem them? Would the Co-op hold me in a back office and call him at work?

No. They just handed over four quid in exchange. No questions asked; the briefest transaction. The mixture of relief and euphoria was intoxicating, only comparable to how I felt when Arsenal won the FA Cup in 1979.

A few days later I took in another book, still expecting my dad to ask where the *blasted Co-op stamp books* had gone. But he didn't and I took the lot, maybe five or six of them. I was flush with cash and elated.

But there were no more books.

The drying up of this revenue stream was difficult for me to manage. I was addicted to the accumulation, and the cash offered an illusion of independence.

No one at school ever talked about money; we didn't really want anything, nothing was marketed at us in the way brands target kids today. I had my own reasons to want money but otherwise the subject didn't come up. We knew what money could buy and it was unimpressive. A boy in my year received a digital watch for his bar mitzvah, and demonstrated it as if we would be envious. He'd misjudged his audience. The watch would only tell you the time if you pushed a button to light up its digits, so not only was it worse than any of ours, it amounted to a step backwards from the earliest days of the wristwatch, when it was designed to keep the hands free in battle, notably during World War One. But this boy acted as if he was the envy of his peers, when in fact my humble Timex was better because:

1. It displayed the date (though you had to adjust it manually five times a year).
2. The hands glowed in the dark (for half a minute after the bedroom light was switched off).
3. It was water resistant to 50m (though you wouldn't risk it in the bath).

It was also a rare thing for anyone to mention the future. One boy said he was going to study law as he'd heard you could earn thirty-five thousand pounds a year doing that, but another said he wouldn't spend three years at University when he could work at an insurance firm for fifteen thousand a year instead, and if Higher Education was going to cost him forty-five thousand pounds it was *not worth it*. I felt that the first boy was probably on to something, which has proved to be the case as he is rich today and the other one isn't, but I didn't want to be either of them. I needed quick cash for the accumulation of small things.

La nueva dama opened her mouth, and her eyes fell at the

sides in anguish. My hand was now out of the bag, I hadn't taken anything, but I didn't know what she was going to do next. We were not friends. This must have been a grim gig for her, these ungrateful English children taking their meals for granted and showing no interest in her, asking no questions. What was wrong with them? Something must have been building in her because after a second or two of stand-off, she lost it:

'He's a thief, he's a thief, *you are a thief!*'

It was as if she was sounding the alarm, out in the village square, warning of horse thieves like a character in a Cormac McCarthy novel. And someone did come: my brother, roused by the shouting. The pitch and tone of a voice from another land was unusual, but it was saying the same thing that had been said of me many times, because I had stolen from everyone nearby, and anyone who came to the house needed to keep an eye on their belongings. My brother was sick of me, and when he entered, ostensibly as Dad's representative at the crime scene, he wore a look of disgust. Perhaps he'd learned that from his father but it came without the counterpoint that Dad would often employ, when he would bend our relationship the other way, adopt a sad expression, look down at the floor near my feet and say:

'You hate me, don't you?'

I'd protest that I didn't hate him, but he was not a person who tolerated any contradiction, so he'd thin out his voice somehow, and clip the end of the sentence, so that I knew I was not to reply, and he'd say:

'You *hate* me.'

He really sounded the *t* in hate, to let me know that I was a bad and ungrateful child.

My brother, partly through his devotional loyalty to his

sole remaining parent (and possibly because he regretted telling me the combination for his red plastic money box, with dials on the front like a safe), had a low opinion of me: 'You're just a thief,' he said, 'a thief.'

I said that I'd only been looking to see if the tea lady had any Green Shield Stamps in her handbag that I could stick in an incomplete book. This might have washed when I was seven or eight but I was fourteen. Though my lie did not dissuade her from her first, correct, conclusion, that I was a thief, it did serve to placate her somehow, to slow her down, so I stuck with the Green Shield Stamps story, ignored my brother as he stalked out of the kitchen, and the tea lady subsequently resigned her position.

Perhaps my lie had proved effective because it was supported by my status as a junior philatelist. I had been collecting since 1977 when I acquired (probably with stolen money) a mint set of the Queen's Silver Jubilee stamps. I still have them if you're interested; I'm always willing to cash in stamps.

I collected in the style of the accumulator that I was, ripping or steaming the stamp from any letter I found. Foreign ones were best and they didn't have to be mint or unused. Dad gave me the odd used stamp but one look in his chest of drawers told me he had many more pink 2½p ones on stacks of old letters. I went into that drawer, without asking, and removed all those pink stamps from the envelopes. One of each was never enough. I imagined they were worth money for a start, and this was a bumper haul.

My dad came into my room one night and asked me if I'd torn the stamps off the letters in his drawer. I'd have said no if I thought I was going to be in trouble but my stamp collecting was a parentally approved hobby.

He said that all those letters were from Mummy.

Only now do I realise that for Dad, Mum was much more a dead *wife* than a dead *mother*. It was as if his was the greater loss, almost as if, in his mind, events *only* happened to him.

He said he could no longer tell which letters came when, as the dates were on the franking on the stamps. He said this with a sadness that I understood I'd caused. I'd irreparably spoiled something that was beyond precious with characteristic thoughtlessness.

The headmaster at my primary school was fond of a science demonstration in assembly. He would heat up a gallon oil can with just a little water in it to the point where it was steaming, and then seal it. As it cooled the can would abruptly contract with a crack and a twisting of metal, collapsing inwards due to the forces acting on it, as the hot gases inside reacted. It was impressive, although I can't remember how he supplied heat. A cigarette lighter possibly. There was an air of danger, partly because he looked uncertain throughout.

As I thought about my mum's letters I felt like the can shrinking inwards. Air could pass through my mouth and throat but not to my lungs. My heart began to pinball around. Dad was impassive. I was the most selfish, uncaring son anyone could have.

I don't know where all those stamps are now but I could find them. There's a phrase you often hear people use: 'It's here somewhere.' Everything I've ever valued is here somewhere, close to where I'm sitting. Unfortunately the accumulating of physical objects does not displace bad memories.

*

The 2½p stamp replaced the 6d (sixpence) stamp on Decimalisation Day, February 15th 1971. Inevitably there was a postal strike at the time, so the new stamps only came into circulation on 8 March, two days after I turned five.

When my mum used the new pink 2½p stamps it was because she was sending second-class letters between March 1971 and her death on August 22nd 1972. All those letters to Dad with the pink stamps on must have been written from St Margaret's Hospital. I didn't read them; they just passed through my hands.

Following my research about the stamps, and the writing of all these pages, I had an urge to look for Mum's letters, something I hadn't thought to do my whole life. I contacted my stepmother and arranged to visit her, at a time when she was alone in the house. I hadn't been back there since she gave me the PG Tips carrier bag.

We chatted for a while and then I told her I wanted to look for anything to do with my mum, particularly any letters she wrote. My stepmother said that she 'shouldn't have done it' but she'd once read one of Mum's letters to Dad, in which she had written: 'Did you ever really love me?'

There was a tightening in my chest and I asked her where she'd seen that letter, and she said in Dad's room. I went upstairs to look in the drawer where he kept his letters when I was a boy. All I found was some correspondence between Mum and various hotels that she'd booked for family holidays, among them Tenby in 1971 and Lyme Regis in 1972. I remember the day we were told she wouldn't be coming to Lyme Regis with us, because she wasn't well enough. I cried and cried. A letter from the Hotel Buena Vista showed the booking was for

August 4–15th 1972. She died a week after we came home. Perhaps she was waiting for us.

I searched elsewhere in the room, through the cupboards where the porn had been hidden, through filing cabinets of financial paperwork, and through a desk drawer filled with pages of obsessive golf diaries. No letters. Then I noticed his bedside cabinet.

It was not the wooden cupboard that he'd kept his girlie magazines in when I was a boy, but an MDF cabinet with drawers. I pulled open the top one and noticed some familiar envelopes that were missing stamps. They were addressed to my dad, care of the Hotel Buena Vista. I stared at them and then carefully slipped out the writing paper inside. Between the dates Mum had written on the letters and the visible part of the franking on the envelope that hadn't been torn off by a stamp collector, it was clear on which date each one had been written.

There was also one letter with no address on the envelope, just *Roy*, which she must have given to someone who visited her so they could pass it to my dad. It's dated February 8th, presumably 1972, and is also written from hospital. It reads:

Dearest Darling,

Dr Medley saw me this morning. He said I am making progress but it is <u>very</u> slow. He didn't say I needed any more platelets.

I said how long would it be ... he said at the rate I'm going it will be two more weeks, but I am definitely making slow progress.

He said I would be able to go back to normal when I got out but I would have to rest a bit if I got tired.

This was the first time I'd learned the name of one of the doctors who cared for Mum. I have no memory of her being in hospital at that time. The blood cell mutation must have occurred early that year or perhaps in 1971. My Uncle Geoff, Mum's brother-in-law who emigrated to Australia with her sister, once told me that Mum found me 'a handful' when I was five, and that he and Hazel realised much later that she must have been weakening with leukaemia before her diagnosis.

I wouldn't have understood why she was less able to smile, or to laugh. Perhaps I began to try harder to please her, making things worse.

There are no further letters until three that were written from Almond Ward, St Margaret's Hospital, to the Hotel Buena Vista, on 5th, 7th, and 13th August 1972. They are generally cheerful in tone, with nice stories about having *a good laugh* when visited by her neighbours Hazel, whose children went to Staples Road and who lived a few doors from my friend Luke, and Doreen, who lived next door to my now stepmother, across the street. What is most striking, though, is the confirmation that she did not know she was dying. On Saturday August 5th she wrote:

> *My spleen is still rather swollen and uncomfortable and I rather suspect it might have something to do with why the last transfusions weren't very successful, so as there is only Mum to go home to I shall stay here until it is right down.*

On Monday August 7th she wrote:

> *My own dearest darling,*
> *It was lovely to get your letter and the children's cards*

this morning. I have felt so low since you went and missed you
dreadfully. I'm sorry you had to wait for my letter but they gave
me a painkiller on Friday for my spleen and it made me so
ill – (why do I only ever get the side effects and not the results)
visiting time with my mother and your parents was purgatory …

I think about you all the time and picture you on the beach
with bats and balls. It is such hard work on your own but I
bet the children are loving every minute of it. Don't do the
washing except pyjamas, let them wear dirty socks and pants –
who cares! I hope you find a kind chambermaid to help you.

… The last 10 years have been happy ones darling and this
is our first real trouble. I am going to get better and next year
we will have a happy time together again. You are marvellous
taking them by yourself. I hope you get a few early nights and
some lovely food, at least you won't have to cook breakfast,
and you weren't always so keen on the evening stroll! Dearest
darling enjoy yourselves and come back to another Medley
miracle. Lots of love and kisses to you all.

Dr Medley must have known long before then that there
was nothing he could do, but the decision had perhaps
already been taken not to tell her that she was terminally
ill. It saddens me to pick up notes of irritation about her
own mum, my Granny Price, who would have been twisted
up inside with the knowledge she was watching her daughter die while having to go along with this crazy charade that
she would be home soon, purgatory for all concerned.

On Sunday August 13th Mum wrote a final letter:

My darling Hubble,
Sorry to disappoint you but I won't be out on Tuesday when
you come home. My temp is still up and down like a yo-yo and

*my spleen is still up altho' not painful, but I had a severe pain
the other side, which is better now thanks to some less severe
painkillers. However I have been rather grim to-day with a
high temp, so goodness knows when I'll come home.*

*I should let them take the children on the cheap mid week
fares, they can go for ¼ fare.*

*If I feel better tomorrow I will add to this. Sorry it's so
miserable. I do love and miss you all.*

I'm not sure who was organising the train travel for us
or who we went with. I know that Dad had driven down
because on August 5th she had written:

*It said in the paper there was a lot of traffic so I hope the
journey wasn't too bad.*

The last letter looks to be signed *Poddy* but I don't know
if that's correct. Mum and Dad seem to have had a variety
of pet names for one another, most of which are hard to
make out in her handwriting.

I couldn't find anything that said 'Did you ever really
love me?' and wonder what my stepmother saw, or if she'd
misremembered. She was eighty-five then and feeling very
unwell after an operation. Somewhere in that house, up in
the loft, maybe, there might be more letters, possibly some
from my dad to Mum, and perhaps the postcards we sent
to her, but these ones from the hospital kept next to Dad's
bed are clearly of special importance.

We came home from Lyme Regis and Mum died seven
days later. Who knows why Dad took us away when she was
so close to death, or why he didn't want to be at her bedside? Who knows if they could tell how long she had left?

I told my sister about the letters and she said she'd like to see them. I scanned them all and sent an email expressing my frustration that Mum's condition was kept from her. After she had read them she wrote back to say that there were two ways of looking at it. Either that Mum had 'died positively', believing she would go on holiday with us the following year, or that she would have died 'desperately sad', knowing she'd never see us grow up.

I'm not convinced 'she died positively', because I don't see it as a case of know the truth and die sad or be told a lie and die happy. There was a third possibility, that she would have been able to cope with a terminal prognosis, and that it would have allowed her to write the letters that knowledge would have prompted, to have informed conversations with her parents, perhaps her children too, and to have phoned her sister. All those people were also denied the chance to say goodbye.

I considered writing an email back to my sister in which I would speculate whether the people herded into gas chambers by the Nazis could be said to have 'died positively', believing they were going to have a shower. But I didn't want to hurt her feelings with a false and unhelpful analogy. We both lost our mum.

I have come to realise that no one sees the world quite the way you do. Even with a great deal of shared experience there is always a shift of a few degrees in perspective, and no one's pain is ever the same as yours.

I also realise now that the Co-op stamp books hadn't been left behind by Mum but by the housekeepers. They stuck the stamps in while I was at school, which was why I'd never seen the books. So they didn't have a trace of Mum on them. Taking them to the supermarket wasn't a betrayal. I hadn't been holding something she'd held, running my fingers over stamps that she'd licked and stuck into place, maybe some of them had been put in by Emma, but not by Mum.

Her stamps were all those little pink ones, costing the equivalent of a sixpence a time. Opening the clasp on her purse, which my little fingers could never budge, and handing over the coins, perhaps in the post office on Loughton High Road, which is now a pub called The Last Post. If it were November she'd keep a sixpence back for the Christmas pudding and whoever found it in their bowl could hope for good luck in the New Year. It's a tradition that's all but died out. Nowadays most puddings are shop bought, the sixpences were melted down in 1980, and people have had to come up with new ideas about how luck is allocated. The more logical theories consider geography, skin pigmentation and gender.

Mum would have made our Christmas pudding in her kitchen, and she'd have put a sixpence in, I'm sure, as her mum would have done before her. Granny Price would certainly have made her own pudding too, in between inspections of her beetroot crop.

So it's quite possible that I found a sixpence in my helping of Christmas pudding when I was a little boy, and Mum and I would have shared beaming smiles of joy. But I only recall finding it once, in a pudding made by my Auntie Carol. I remember the thrill of it, aged about ten, the smiles all around their big table, from my place at the lower children's table at the end. I can't remember any good luck coming from it. I had the feeling that it was just a bit of dinner-table fun (like being told that sprouts made your hair curl or cabbage gave you a hairy chest), and I did not pick up, either from those around me or from some twinge inside, that given the luck I'd had so far the coin coming to me was, if anything, deeply ironic.

Songs

Mum sat up on pillows in her hospital bed and was always a bit too high to get to. There were usually other adults there so I felt restricted. It was exciting to see her but there was to be no noise or exuberance, and there was never enough time to calm down and just sit with her, or to start doing something that she could oversee. Parents sometimes like to watch or just be near to their children playing, they don't always have the strength or the know-how to join in, especially when they are tired, or dying.

The only time I recall being alone with her, when she was ill, she drew a picture of a cat for me, looking out through some French windows like the ones we had at home. It was a pencil drawing seen from behind the cat so you couldn't see its face. Perhaps that was the last time I saw her; perhaps that was why I was alone with her. I don't know if she had a cat when she was younger or if she'd have liked one for us.

Some years later my sister wanted a cat. Before long a pair of entertaining kittens appeared. Dad had dogs as a boy and the way he loved pets, together with the way he adored his school and the Cub Scouts, even his enthusiasm for the war, showed that childhood was his happiest time.

He was most content when talking to or about our pets and once he'd remarried he was never without a Golden Retriever for the next thirty years.

He indulged these animals, feeding them from the table with his fingers so they'd stay at his side. His constant praising of them, talking up their qualities, real or imagined, was revealing in that he did not speak of his children or grandchildren in the same way. He'd say that his dog was 'always smiling, always smiling', and no one knew how to respond. And no one smiled when he said it, which was his point perhaps; people did not wag their tails for him anywhere near enough for his liking. In truth, we all wagged all the time.

When I took my daughter, aged two, to his house for a visit, I went out on to the patio to take a phone call about work and while I was gone she approached her grandad in his armchair because he was stroking a Yorkshire terrier. The dog jumped forward and bit her in the face. When I came back into the room seconds later he remained in his chair with the dog on his lap while my little girl stood to one side crying, with blood streaming from her cheek. It pains me to this day that I failed to protect her from him. I've always been unable to maintain boundaries around myself in the face of his various behaviours but to leave her alone with him, even for a minute, was a disastrous mistake. There is, thankfully, no scar. The only consequence is that my daughter is scared of dogs, but not grandfathers.

Our hospital visits to Mum seemed infrequent. Our house resembled the Home Front, while a battle was being waged by the doctors at St Margaret's. We lived in an unreal atmosphere, with a spirit of mucking in, of digging for victory, the true horrors of the conflict kept from the innocents at home.

We would go to Sainsbury's in Debden on a Saturday morning with a list written by Mum. I suppose we started doing that before she died, we certainly continued it long after she had gone, with the exact same piece of lined paper.

This was a time when the tasks I was given, such as looking for things on the shelves at the supermarket, made me feel part of the coping, as if I was doing my bit. I would help find items in Bejam, the frozen food store, where a good memory for what was in each freezer was essential since they didn't have clear tops and you had to lift every lid to see inside. I could remember where everything was and it pleased me to please Dad. He bought sliced beef in gravy, boil-in-the-bag casseroles, frozen peas, fish fingers and Arctic Roll, which was the best thing in the shop.

Dad didn't know how to cook anything, and the rich resources of our back garden nurtured by Mum – her tomatoes, runner beans, the rhubarb, the blackberries and cooking apples for stewing and baking – all went to ruin after she died.

But we settled into a routine for breakfast and Dad grilled sausages and bacon each morning. He didn't seem to mind that my brother wanted baked beans and I wanted Alphabetti Spaghetti to go with our meat. I didn't mind that the tinned pasta was dried out and congealed by the time it left the pan, or that breakfast was exactly the same each day. My sister wisely had jam on bread every morning.

The kitchen I'd spent so many hours in, playing round Mum's feet, was changing for ever. For lunch each Saturday, Dad would boil a large cylindrical ham, and a big pan of potatoes, for twenty minutes exactly, measured by a ticking kitchen timer. Only when it buzzed were the potatoes tipped into a colander in clouds of steam. They'd usually disintegrated so were easy to mash with slabs of butter. It didn't matter that they now had no flavour since there would be a gravy boat with an Oxo cube dissolved in boiling water.

Dad always threw salt over his shoulder for luck and then all over his food the moment it was in front of him, before tasting it. I grew up thinking salt cooled food down when it was too hot to eat. In the summer he would have a pile of salt on his plate into which he would dip radishes.

On school mornings we were among the twelve million people who listened to Terry Wogan on Radio 2, and laughed at his imagined life of the Director General of the BBC, 'the DG', roaming the rooftop at Broadcasting House. Wogan talked about the BBC1 show *Dallas* so much that we had to start watching it on Saturday nights to see what he was on about. The episode revealing 'who shot JR' was seen by twenty-one million people in Britain (and eighty million in America). The shooter was J. R. Ewing's beautiful lover Kristin, played by Mary Crosby, daughter of Bing. Dad adored Bing, of course, but appeared not to notice Mary.

While the ham was boiling he would play Max Bygraves records. The *SingalongaMax* albums featured nostalgic old songs, and he would duly singalong or whistle deafeningly. Presumably he was being transported back to his childhood when 'Daisy, Daisy, give me your answer do' and 'Won't you come home, Bill Bailey' were popular. It was wholesome family entertainment, even though the Daisy referred to was Daisy Greville, the Countess of Warwick, who was a mistress of Edward VII.

Max Bygraves exploited his family entertainer tag, and earned the role as host of *Family Fortunes* on television, yet he quietly had three children from affairs outside his marriage, as well as three more with his wife.

The singalong albums may have been inspired by similar recordings released by Bing Crosby, who is said to have sold half a billion records. Crosby is referred to in Bygraves's 1974 hit 'Back in My Childhood Days', which was a favourite of Dad's, packed as it is with references to so many things familiar to Londoners of the thirties, forties and fifties. Dad could scarcely credit that Bygraves (who had taken the name Max from the comedian Max Miller) had written the words himself. Listening to it now the line that catches my ear is:

We joined the Boy Scouts or we grew up as louts

The Scouts had a veneer of respectability, good people doing good things, which fostered camaraderie and community spirit. They would knock on doors in bob-a-job week looking for things to do for a bob (a shilling). Then you could display a bob-a-job card in your window (to show that you'd been pestered once and wanted to be left alone). From a young age they swore allegiance to the Queen, earned badges for skills learned, and promised to do their best, in an improbable attempt at continual goodness.

It transpired that the upstanding façade masked a hidden culture of bullying and sexual abuse. When I became suspicious that my dad's love of Scouting was associated with his love of teen flesh, I discovered that the Scout Association has paid out over half a million pounds to victims of sexual assault going back to the Second World War. Yet the

Bygraves lyric reveals the esteem in which the Scouts were held, as upright citizens, leaving them universally entrusted to take boys into their care.

Those strange times, particularly the war years in the face of the common Nazi enemy, had an atmosphere all of their own, and that singalong music took a generation back there in the nineteen seventies. 'Happy Days Are Here Again', 'Don't Dilly Dally on the Way', 'It's a Long Way to Tipperary', on and on they went. Start one up in any war-time concert hall, or air-raid shelter, or Scout 'Gang Show' where everyone is 'Riding along on the crest of a wave', and you can picture people singing together.

As for the entertainers themselves, a private life can be at odds with the public image. That certainly appeared the case with Crosby and Bygraves. The public face of an organisation can mask its private side too, and the dignified public face of a parent affords the same opportunity for a hidden life at home.

Dad sometimes mentioned that Frankie Vaughan, a popular singer in the fifties, was one of Mum's 'favourites', though he rarely approved of her taste, putting a little sneer in his voice when he mentioned Vaughan or Richard Burton or the movie star Alan Ladd, who I'm supposedly named after. Ladd was always standing on a box, according to Dad, because of his height.

Vaughan managed to stay married for forty-eight years until his death, reportedly resisting the advances of Marilyn Monroe when they made a film together. He was known for giving money to Boys' Clubs and for trying to help kids who had joined gangs – boys outside the Scouts, you can assume. He was described as a man who was loved for himself as well as his talent, which included some dramatic high-kicking during songs. I don't know which of his recordings Mum liked. The only song I remember her singing is 'Yes! We Have No Bananas', which was another wartime favourite. No one sings that any more, but if I ever hear a snatch of it I picture our back door open and Mum's voice singing as she pegged out the washing.

Holes

Yet what can one poor voice avail
Against three tongues together?

LEWIS CARROLL

There was nowhere good to hide in Dulles Airport. Which was all it had in common with our house. It occupies twelve thousand acres, or more than eighteen square miles, of the state of Virginia, and serves nearby Washington, DC. Home was a four-bedroom house with gardens front and rear, occupying about a quarter of an acre of Loughton, which in part serves London as a green-belt commuter town and takes up six square miles for its population of thirty thousand. Twice that many people pass through Dulles every day.

It was hard to get lost at home. You could lock yourself in the toilet, or go to the bottom of your bed beneath the covers or under the bed or into the cupboard under the stairs (though once its latch clicked shut you were stuck in there), or up into the loft, but none of these places would keep you hidden for long, not with three other people in the house.

Now those same three would be scouring Dulles looking for me. Ironically, the one I'd punched in the face would be least likely to join the hunt. She'd be sticking close to her dad. What I'd done this time felt climactic.

I needed a hidey-hole.

Is that why *Alice in Wonderland* is so popular, because everyone longs to drop down a rabbit hole where they will meet nothing familiar, and no one notices they've gone? Didn't Alice appear to wander off in the first place because her sibling wasn't interested in her?

But I didn't need a fantasy, I wasn't dreaming, I was a teenager on the run from my family. I needed an escape. Panic fixes you in the present like a small child or an animal, making planning impossible. I could see nothing past the objects and people in my field of vision. It didn't even occur to me to look for exits. I saw a café but imagined I'd be ejected without any money to spend, and it felt too exposed in any case; they'd spot me in there. I wanted to hide behind something and still be able to see. There were so many people going in all directions, it was as if I was the only one standing still, but moving would make it harder to keep watch. I might not see my family before they saw me. I didn't take off the New York Mets cap that I'd worn ever since we went to Shea Stadium for a baseball game the week before. It didn't occur to me that they might be looking out for my hat as well as for me. I felt in my pocket for my little red plastic dragon that I always had in my school trousers, but I hadn't taken it on holiday. There was just a coin in there, a quarter, so I held that instead. What if they had just stayed in the seats we were sitting in when it happened? I'd lost track of where those seats were, and that felt like returning to the scene of the crime, meaning I'd be caught. I could have hidden in the toilets but they all had cleaners going in and out and it would only be a dead end.

At home you could hide in the Wendy house at the top of our garden, though you could be seen from the house the whole way up there, past Mum's rockery and the ash tree and the apple trees and the painted wooden goalposts that leant over sideways.

Near the compost heap was an empty garden shed with lining paper in faded yellow, pink and green. We called it The Wendy House. It smelt of damp wood and spiders. My sister played in there on her own or with the two little girls from over the road, whose mother was so kind to her when our mum died. My brother and I would be on the lawn playing football or cricket, games thought not to be for girls, who might join in tennis or badminton, when boys were expected to play nicely, and never to whack a shuttlecock straight at them.

I often imagined a space under the floor of that Wendy house, with only enough room for me to lie on my front reading *The Famous Five*. On all sides of me would be shelves filled with books. The ceiling would be low over my head. Nobody would ever know about this undiscoverable haven. I didn't consider the practicalities of the excavation, or the damp, or how I would get in there, never mind how it would be lit or heated or ventilated. It was more of a hidey-hole than a jailbreak fantasy.

The men who escaped from Colditz imagined different lives outside the prison, but they were pragmatists, not fantasists, who worked out how to make things they needed (keys, maps, tools, a glider), and how to distract their captors long enough to get away (clay heads on their pillows). But they also had the reassuring knowledge that there was somewhere else waiting for them. They wanted to go home.

Escaping *to* home is very different to escaping *from* home.

We could all agree that, if you don't make it, there are worse things than starting afresh in wartime Switzerland, but a new life in Washington, DC in the eighties, without forged papers, local currency or a disguise? How was that to happen?

I'd been sitting next to my sister in the departure lounge. She was twelve, without her mum for nine years nearly to the day. Her brown hair was cut to shoulder length; she was thin, a little anxious, in thrall to her father, and with brothers not on speaking terms.

When she and I argued, I had to take the blame for it, since Dad saw her as defenceless, another manifestation of his attitude to women and girls. He taught us that before a tennis match you spin a racket to decide who serves. Our old wooden rackets had a rough and smooth side at the base of the strings. So one person called rough or smooth, as in heads or tails. He also taught us that the polite thing to do, in a mixed game, is to invite a lady to call. Our lives were peppered with this kind of etiquette and, as I rarely missed a chance to identify bias against me, it drove me crazy that my sister was *always* the one asked, 'Rough or smooth?' Once when she answered 'smooth' and the racket landed smooth side up I said:

'I would have said that.'

Not that it matters, as it is literally arguing the toss, but Dad narrowed his eyes and pursed his lips and stared away from me as he strode to the far end of the court, from where he would serve too hard for me to return the ball. His disdain and disappointment saturated the block of air resting over the court so that if his dissatisfaction had a colour (it's orange in my mind), it might be seen as a rectangular prism, tennis-court length and breadth, rising to the height of his oddly effeminate ball toss. I imagine that you can't see into this orange cuboid but you can hear the soundtrack of his displeasure, with no other sounds at all, as if one man was playing himself in a closed-off coloured box, and hating it: 'Come *on* ... pick the *damn* balls up ... *over* the net ... out ... *out* ... out *again* ... *never* return a serve that is long, that's very rude ... that's long ... long ... long *again* ... How *on earth* you manage to get it over the damn fence I just *do not know* ... go and *find* it ... *I don't know*, you hit the *damn* thing ... *look for it!*'

This usually took place on the Ridgeway Park public courts in Chingford. He wouldn't take us to his Tennis Club until we could at least hit a ball in the face of his solemnity.

After one telling-off by our dad, when my sister's uncor-roborated version of events had been rubber-stamped as usual, I was left seething with injustice and stood outside her bedroom impotently throwing V-signs with both hands. She wasn't in there, I thought no one else was upstairs, but Dad was behind me. Grabbing my upper arm, he smacked my bare legs a few times and left without a word. I went to my room so no one would see me crying. I never saw him hit my brother or sister.

At Dulles the four of us had been waiting for our flight, sitting in a row of seats fixed to the floor. I was looking at pictures of tennis players in a magazine with my sister (her Chris Evert, me John McEnroe), while I said silly things to make her giggle. Then Dad spoke to her:

'What's he *doing now?*'

His impatient tone signalled to her that the family boat was pulling away from the dock and she'd better get on board or be left on the quayside with me. Adopting his weary tone she said:

'He's just being stupid.'

I thought we'd been having fun. Why did she hop onside with him just like that? But perhaps she meant I was just being daft. I realise, only as I write this, that she may have been trying to placate him, saying there was nothing to worry about.

Unfortunately, my injustice reflex prompted me to swing my hand up from by my side and clout her in the mouth, as if my arm was a rake and she'd stepped on the end. I felt the back of my fingers impact against her lips and teeth; her arms were down, she was taken by surprise. I was on my feet, ready to go for them all. My brother stood up and was going to say something, Dad too was out of his chair, they were all shocked, and then I pulled the pin:

'You're a poof! You come in to my room at night and touch me up! You're just a poof. You're a *poof*. You come in to my room!'

It was as if all the other people in the airport were no longer there. Dad just stood still, my brother was staring angrily.

'Don't be *stupid*, shut up, you're being *stupid*,' he said.

I looked at my brother, expecting him to turn to my dad, perhaps questioningly, but there was no flicker of doubt, he just glared at me. Did he not believe me? He couldn't have thought I was making it up? He and my sister stood alongside their dad, the three of them like an unusually hostile all-standing interview panel about to ask: 'And what makes you think you'd be a suitable member of this family going forward?'

Dad didn't speak, he didn't grab my arm, didn't take a swing, there were witnesses all around. And I didn't feel like that boy any more, I was fifteen, I was a terrace season-ticket holder at Arsenal, I smoked Marlboro Red, drank snakebite and vandalised buses. I'd had fourteen detentions in one term at school and was proud of it. I listened to The Jam and The Stranglers and had a copy of 'Too Drunk to Fuck' by The Dead Kennedys (although it was hidden under my turntable). I had decided to activate the untouched detonator that lived with us, to push that T-bar down into the box and blow the bloody doors off.

I couldn't find a way to say I was hurt and sad and lonely. I only knew glaring and rage and shouting, but I tried to change our family story with my revelation. Now I'd said this surely everything would be different; but was my own sting going to finish me, like a bee?

As I turned to go it was as if I'd discharged myself from the ward, ripped the tubes out of my arms, disconnected myself from life support, stolen a white coat and escaped. But I was not like a POW, I had no rendezvous planned, no fixer on the other side of the fence, and I didn't want to go home. There was nowhere to go, and no hole that would open up, letting me fall and fall and fall, to safety. This was me jumping out of the family plane with no parachute.

I found myself by a silver wall somewhere in the airport and turned my head to the side to look back. Not only was I without papers, a convincing outfit and a route to neutral Switzerland, I couldn't even utilise the eighteen square miles of Dulles. I was stuck in the departure lounge facing certain recapture. There would be no applause from the other inmates when I was brought back to my bunk after a few days in the hole. The other inmates were in the search party.

The French Foreign Legion often appeared in my war comics, in their blue tunics and white hats. They offered criminals, or the broken-hearted, the chance to disappear. Perhaps they would accept someone with difficulties at home? After all, many of them had only done what I was doing, they'd run away, and now they sang *Non, je ne regrette rien* on parade together. But I was too young for the Legion. I'd have to think of something else. Perhaps I could do a Reggie Perrin: fake my own death and start afresh?

The Fall and Rise of Reginald Perrin was a comedy series in which the hero's planned disappearance was presented as rational wish-fulfilment. This was a time when working life was called 'the rat race', so that school represented 'the happiest days of your life', unless you were 'posh', meaning you were 'rich', giving you a chance to 'live the high life'. But all this collective discontent didn't often boil over; it was a social volcano kept dormant partly by granting each man the inviolable right to fuck up his own family. That way he could feel powerful enough in his castle to tolerate a bleak job in a cultural vacuum for fifty boring years.

My own fresh start wasn't going well, padding round America in Dunlop Green Flash with every window closed and door secured. I was going to fail at the start like a racehorse stuck in its stall. I could have done with a secret identity, like a superhero, so I could hide in plain sight, and possibly escape from the departure lounge by walking across the ceiling. The silver wall I had my back to was perhaps stainless steel, like the entrance to a kitchen in a café. We were flying home to London so we must have checked our bags in, gone through security (such as it was, twenty years before 9/11) and were waiting for our gate to be called. It wasn't as simple as just passing through a door into the street. Had it been I might have started walking and tried to get by on my skills as a petty thief until I could work something out. I believed there was no way back after what I'd said to Dad. They would all hate me. I'd have to live in America, which would be better than living at home. I saw some payphones, went over to a free one and picked up the receiver, then I shoved my quarter into the slot but there was no one to ring. I stood there for a long time with the receiver to my ear acting as if I was a Mets fan just calling a buddy in Queens.

I don't remember even trying to get out of Dulles. The inevitability of being caught was paralysing. I'm not sure how I would have reacted if my family had boarded their jumbo jet back to London without me, rather than have to pay for new flights later, whether I'd have felt abandoned or released, lost or loose.

Even now the thought of beginning a new life in America from the age of fifteen sometimes feels like a missed opportunity. If I'd been allowed to stay, having managed to both tell my story and be *believed*, then been placed in foster care, I might have settled into a high school, with the motivation to study, graduate and go to college, and work to pay my way, eventually emerging into the state of Virginia, or Maryland or Pennsylvania, as an educated young adult, unfettered by fantasies of hiding under a shed.

All I knew was that Washington, DC was the last stop on our dream three-week fly-drive holiday around America that I had now ruined for everyone. It was where we'd always wanted to go, mainly because of the films and television shows that we loved. None of us knew or cared who John Foster Dulles was (a greatly respected former Secretary of State, worthy of having an Airport named for him despite being referred to by Prime Minister Anthony Eden as Dull, Duller, Dulles). We were there for the Americana, the hamburgers, the baseball caps, the big cars, and the cool accent we all tried to do. Even my dad would attempt to mimic John Wayne saying: 'Get off your horse.'

In Britain some airports are named after popular local heroes of immense talent who have brought pride to their city, despite personal histories of alcohol abuse and domestic violence. In America naming an airport is often an act to commemorate public service. But I didn't know Dulles, I barely knew JFK, I didn't even really know where I was, only that I was attached to three people by some invisible thread that I hadn't broken with my outburst. Then I saw them.

I didn't run, I froze. They'd seen me first and were staring, not coming any closer, and I was powerless to prevent an unconscious drift back into the fold, sullen and unapologetic, as if I was being pulled by a tractor beam, like the *Millennium Falcon* into the Death Star.

I had expected a familiar ritual of serious-faced displeasure, as if I'd been messing about at Chessington Zoo for a while, but this wasn't just another episode of bad behaviour, I'd evidently disturbed them all, I could feel that much, and I realised they wouldn't have boarded our flight without me. We reconvened in silence. No one touched anyone, or expressed concern, relief or anger, as we moved wordlessly to our plane where we occupied four seats across the middle.

I was in an aisle seat next to my dad, where I was surprised to find he was being kind to me, while keeping me from my siblings on the other side of him. They were therefore unable to ask me what I'd been going on about in the airport when I'd called him a poof over and over again, a derogatory term for homosexuals that was, in those days, far worse than the old-fashioned 'queer'.

I was confused about whether my dad was, as people would say then, 'one of them', but clearly something sexual had gone on between us, which he had instigated and controlled, engineering the encounters for his gratification. It was also clear that it was a secret and that telling anyone would be a disaster for my personal reputation (so it might be best if you could keep it under your hat that you've read this, thanks).

It's important to be clear that what my father did to me was not a consequence of an apparently repressed homosexuality. It's not inevitable if you are gay that you will molest and abuse boys any more than a straight man will inevitably molest his daughter. These two things must not be conflated. Adults, gay, straight or of any orientation, do not normally become sexually aroused by children. The child molester acts on fantasies of control, manipulation and power. Sex is not irrelevant but it's frequently not the prime mover in these acts.

Furthermore, it is hard to properly assess what my father's sexual preferences were, or are. Initially he molested me when I was pre-pubescent, as if paedophilic fantasies were being enacted, but he then installed housekeepers into the family home perhaps in part to protect himself from his own urges. He subsequently molested me again when I was pubescent, amounting to hebephilia, an interest in children aged eleven to fourteen. But his porn collection shows an astonishing obsession with teenage boys who appear post-pubescent, putting him in the ephebophile camp. Were there any adult same-sex experiences? Who knows?

Not long after we were back home from America, Dad made an unexpected appearance in my room while I was lying in bed. It had been a while since he'd done that. He began to talk about our neighbour over the road. He said that if she hugged her daughters, it didn't make her a lesbian.

He phrased it as a question:

'That doesn't make her a lesbian, does it?' he said.

I was obligated to concur, to go along with the inference that it was as absurd to consider her a lesbian as it was to call him a poof.

And that was that. He was trying to say he had just been hugging me like a mum with her daughters. He didn't say whether the daughters were stripped naked for this hug or whether the mum was only in her underpants or whether the girls were told that this was a 'special cuddle' that they weren't to tell anyone about. But it was clear that nothing more was going to be said about the events at the airport. I was muzzled. His story would always be that he had cuddled me only as an affectionate parent, and, most importantly of all, he was no more a homosexual than the lovely mother of two who looked after my little sister. The hurt and anger I'd expressed did not exist. Of course he knew that coerced nudity is not the norm between a parent and a child, and that's why it wasn't mentioned in our little chat.

I understood then that he knew that he was a predatory criminal and that he would continue to manipulate the feelings of two of his children so they would not object to the ostracising of the third, his victim, the one they were supposed to ignore.

Buses

When I went to report my dad to the police for Historic Special Cuddles, I took the bus. I was on Old Street, from where the 55 goes to Hanover Square and my lawyer's office.

I was not a schoolboy, I was fifty-one, five years older than my dad had been the last time he molested me. Having three children of my own had helped me to reflect on what had taken place. It is impossible to imagine even wanting to undress and fondle one of them, then telling them to keep it a secret from the others. There is a bright light generated by the love I feel for them and the love I witness between them and their mother, and it's as if it shines in all directions, so there are no dark corners, even reaching back through the shadows of the past, illuminating more clearly than ever the wickedness I was subjected to and helping me to find the strength to have one last go at confronting it.

The police were coming to me. I had an appointment. I would not be wandering in off the street to consult a desk sergeant, or more likely a civilian, a copper's community helper assigned to be first point of contact, while actual Po-lice are struggling not to be submerged under a crime wave, empowered to use their professional judgement only as they are held to account under the continued monitoring of safeguarding and welfare performance assessments.

I sat on the top deck.

I was alone and the experience was redolent of journeys I made as a teenager when I'd sit up the back to smoke fags and graffiti the backs of the seats with shoplifted marker pens of red, green and blue.

My journey was spent looking out of the window, a valuable practice in any solitary period, now becoming a lost art in the age of the smart phone, the calming thought-rich indolence of the bus passenger, gazing through the glazing, allowing the dust to settle on thoughts, or a mental fog to clear, and new ideas to show green shoots. Memories can turn up at these times, too, some unwanted, of course, hello Daddy, and some too few and far between, hello Mummy.

I hunched my shoulders and kept my face low. I don't talk to strangers on buses, which is customary in London, but I don't want an empty bus, that's disconcerting; it's nice to have people there, to form a collective in case someone falls over, or leaves a glove on a seat, or is in danger of sleeping past their stop. It's preferable to have a few other people on board, though not sharing my seat. Most of the passengers stare at their phones throughout, though there is often one yelling into theirs in a language I can't identify and wish I could understand.

Since I found out about my father's obsession with naked boys, thereby being forced to reassess my childhood at his caressing hands, I'd been walking on the inside of pavements, looking down, as if I might be pounced on. An unsettled feeling stayed with me everywhere I went. Now more than ever I was stuck in a deep furrow of sadness I had no control over, feeling like soiled, tarnished goods, inevitably preoccupied only with my own misfortune.

Looking out of the window I remembered being thrown off a big red bus like this when I was twelve, not for writing on it, which came later, but for printing my own ticket. It wasn't a facsimile created to bunk the fare, but an actual ticket from the driver's electric machine. There used to be a grey button they would hit to eject a slip of paper once you'd put coins in their little dish. Oddly it was the other side of the machine from the driver so he would have to reach his fingers over to touch it. He'd set the fare on his side and then shoot. The button was easy to reach for the waiting passenger, a temptation. I asked for a half to Woodford, please, produced my fare and then, before he could finish his action, jabbed his button. I was quick on the draw, showing off to my peers.

How impressed they must have been when he gave me back my ten pence, along with the ticket, and said:

'Go on, get off.'

I was surprised but I didn't protest. I'd tested his tolerance and overdone it. My friends all trooped off the bus with a few choice words for the driver and we waited for the next one.

If you believe that then I'd politely suggest you haven't been paying attention. I was a very leavable child, reeking of victimhood and inadequacy, not things that bring out empathy in boys, quite the opposite. So I stood alone at the bus stop while they ran up the stairs to the back window. It didn't occur to me to raise a protest, something like: 'Are none of you wankers even going to wait with me?'

No, I reverted to type, the ostracised outsider, necessarily comfortable alone. At least I wouldn't be harshly judged by my peers for a while, though there is also less laughing when you're by yourself.

We were all a bit excitable because we were going to the Woodford ABC to see *Grease*. When I arrived the lights were already down in the vast auditorium and I couldn't see my friends. I assumed they weren't looking out for me and sat on my own.

Grease, a musical set in an all-white California high school in the fifties, was dominating popular culture in 1978. Back then a single that made it to number one in the charts was usually there for a week or two, but the two big hits from that film ('Summer Lovin'' and 'You're the One That I Want') were number one for a combined sixteen weeks. Several other songs from the soundtrack made the top ten, and it seemed everyone saw the film, even my dad. I saw it five times.

Dad took the whole family. It was a surprising outing. Usually we'd be taken to films he wanted to see, like *The Man with the Golden Gun* (I was eight and came out of the South Woodford Plaza humming the James Bond theme and pretending to be Roger Moore). We saw *Zulu Dawn* (when thousands of warriors drummed their shields with their spears we learned nothing about colonialism, only that black people were terrifying) and *Jaws*, which was so frightening that I told my sister I would never be scared of anything ever again. Demonstrating the scepticism that was to become her calling card, she said:

'You probably will be.'

At one point in *Grease*, student Rizzo (played brilliantly by Stockard Channing, despite her being thirty-three) tells a friend that she has 'skipped a period'.

I thought she'd missed a lesson, since we called them

periods at school, but when I'd seen the film previously I felt I'd missed something at this point so I whispered to my dad:

'Does that mean she's missed a lesson?'

There was the briefest moment before he answered, which told me something was afoot and I wished I hadn't asked.

'No, that's a *very* rude joke,' he said.

'Oh yes, I get it,' I said.

My fourteen-year-old brother was grinning.

'No you don't,' he said.

And I didn't. The joke was lost on me. I still thought she'd missed a class and couldn't see the funny side. Rizzo and her friends do not consult a timetable throughout the film. Is that the joke? That *of course* she's missed a lesson, she's the leader of the Pink Ladies and has therefore arrived at life's pinnacle. I did not know what a period was, or that, in fact, there was no joke at all. Where is the humour? She thinks she's pregnant, by Kenickie of all the degenerates to sacrifice your youth to (or in her case, early middle age). Why say, to your inquisitive twelve-year-old, that a girl telling her friend that she's missed her period is a 'rude joke'? Why not say that she thinks she might be pregnant? Like this:

'She thinks she might be pregnant.'

Now tell him it's not that sort of a period.

'It's not that sort of a period.'

Tell him you'll explain later.

'I'll explain later.'

I doubt Dad could have explained menstrual flow, the expulsion of the womb lining, or anything about fallopian tubes, certainly not that they were discovered by Gabrielle Fallopio and called *Tube* because they looked like a pair of tubas. He would have liked a loud tuba to sound over all questions about that time of the month. I remained ignorant for years.

Grease lazily plays with ideas of the virtuous and the fallen, of what a nice girl and boy look like (cardigans) and what bad boys and girls look like (cigarettes). It has a confusing happy ending where Kenickie is overjoyed to learn that Rizzo isn't pregnant (she's possibly menopausal) and virtuous Sandy dresses like a working girl on Hamburg's Reeperbahn, to let Danny know she is open to new choices.

In this cultural climate, and with no mother, I needed more helpful information about women. My father contributed only these three pieces of advice:

Walk in front of them going downstairs (in case they
     should fall).
Walk on the outside of them on pavements
     (presumably so they won't be splashed by a
     stagecoach passing through effluent).
When phoning about car insurance: 'Ask to speak to
     a man, not some silly woman.'

Like a zoo animal born in captivity, I was oblivious to an alternative world outside.

Dad told no stories, not even about Mum, of their courting or their wedding. I only learned recently, when a relative had some cine film converted to VHS, that my mother didn't wear white at the church on her wedding day, but a blue dress and a pink hat. Another unsolved mystery.

Perhaps there wasn't any courting. She was there in the Scout hut every week and they became friends, and she waited for this young man, tall and dark-haired with a good job, who so enjoyed being with the Cubs and Scouts. As did his father (kindly Grandpa Davies), who threw parties for the boys on the tennis court in his garden. She held on for five years, while her younger sister married before her, then had a baby, and emigrated. Only then did Dad propose, aged thirty, still living with his parents.

To the annoyance of Granny Price, who would have preferred a declaration of love for her eldest girl, he announced the engagement by saying:

'We've decided to beat the tax man.'

The old romantic had doubtless learned that income tax relief for married couples was to be increased in the Finance Act of 1963. Let's get hitched, baby.

There are black-and-white photos of the wedding. In some Dad's smiles look pained, a long way from the excited expression he is wearing in a photo of a big group of largely shirtless teenage boys at a Scout camp in 1947.

I wonder now if my father had a secret (and until 1967, illegal) homosexual life. Could he have done? When gay men were being criminalised in the tens of thousands, many of them entrapped and jailed. When they were obliged to meet in certain cinemas, or 'cottages', or privately in secret, a ready lie always prepared. All those years camping with the Scouts, nights under canvas, in and out of tents, all that teenage masturbation, did you still only look? Did you not find anyone who would show you his? Or move around for you? Kneel up, maybe? Was I really your first boyfriend?

I learned from Dad that life with the Cubs and Scouts and at an all-boys school represents heaven on earth and that women are useful for cooking and cleaning but are otherwise irritating.

This was drip-fed over the years, by the casual assignment of household chores, or by wider cultural representation, absorbed as if through the pores, or inhaled like a gas.

On television:

A woman in an apron was normal,
a man in an apron was HILARIOUS.
A woman in stockings and suspenders was a
    desirable short-term pursuit,
a man in stockings and suspenders was
    HILARIOUS.
A man driving a car was virile, despite his
    silly gloves,
a woman driving a car was HILARIOUS.

By the time I'd grown up and been exposed to the outside world, some of Dad's views on women became alarming. In 1987 when Michael Ryan unearthed his stash of weapons and began shooting people, in what became known as the Hungerford Massacre, Dad asked me:

'What do you think of this chap Ryan?'

I mumbled something about how terrible it was. There were sixteen dead, an unprecedented spree for our islands, the kind of murder-suicide you'd expect in the United States of Firearms.

Among Ryan's victims was his mum, who he lived with and whose house he engulfed in burning petrol in the early stages of the massacre.

'I can understand him killing his mother,' said Dad, 'perhaps she was nagging him or something, but why kill all those strangers?'

This took a moment to sink in but has been bobbing to the surface of my mind ever since.

I can understand him killing his mother.

Was this to tell me that his mum was awful, or that my mum was?

Was he talking about Granny Davies, she of the famous trifle, that I named My Favourite Food in a primary school survey? I wasn't well fed, in the sense of being well read, so choices were limited but that trifle was lovely. There were never enough seats to fit us all round the table in their Chingford bungalow, so she'd bring a white painted stool out of the bathroom. To perch up on that, the envy of my siblings, eating trifle, was literally a high point of my childhood.

Granny Davies dropped dead doing the ironing in 1974. Blown aorta. Probably heard it go pop.

'Dead before she hit the floor, that's how I want to go,' said Granny Price, years later.

But Dad could understand a man peppering his mum with bullets.

BLAM, BLAM, BLAM: 'SHUT UP, MUMMY.'

Dorothy Ryan had come across her twenty-seven-year-old son in the street, wandering among some of his victims while their house was burning beyond, and she'd spoken to him. Did she plead with him? Scold or chastise him? Beg him? He shot her in the legs and abdomen, then in the back while she was face down on the ground, where she fell, finally silent.

Later on, when he was holed up in his old school, he wanted to know from the police how his mother was. They told him. He said killing her had been a mistake. Then he said he wished he'd stayed in bed that morning. Then he killed himself. The assumption was that he underwent a prolonged psychotic episode. It was difficult to say, as the only person who knew him well was his mother. His guns were all legally owned.

From all of that my father assumed Ryan's mother had been nagging him and hers was the only murder that was understandable. But for the killer it appeared to be the only one that prompted remorse.

Dad remains a man whose prejudices loom so large in his mind that facts cannot compete.

He lived at home for thirty years, 'active' in the Scouts the whole time, and eventually married one of the few women he would ever get to speak to, the cub leader, Akela of the 15th Chingford Scouts, my mum. So they moved in together on their wedding day after a guard of honour of Cubs had seen them off. Nine years later she suffered a blood mutation and wasted away.

I stared out of the window of the 55. It starts its route at the Bakers Arms in Walthamstow from where Granny Price would take the bus to Finsbury Town Hall, to go to tea dances with her future husband Fred, not far from the Mount Pleasant Sorting Office where he worked. The route crosses the River Lea where Fred was in a rowing club, and down Mare Street where the great Music Hall stars performed at the Hackney Empire, and, after it reopened in 1986, the best comedians of the eighties and nineties. I boarded at Old Street, which has been there since the Romans settled Londinium, and has borne that name since the twelfth century. It was a clear, bright day; there was no condensation on the windows. As I sat there I thought it was perhaps a bit harsh that I was thrown off that bus in 1978. The driver could have just chastised me with withering sarcasm:

'You can press a button. Well done you. Aren't you clever? A proper little Brainbox? No, you are an irritating little prick and I wish to fuck I was allowed to belt you.'

Bus conductors were usually more amiable but these new one-man buses left the driver without his friend, the one who issued the tickets and fielded all the questions about where the hospital was, or the cemetery, or the Green Man pub where they had strippers performing on a Sunday lunchtime (is that rude?).

The driver just used to listen out for the bell: one ding to stop, two to go. Now if there was trouble on the journey – some drunken nonsense, or a medical emergency – the driver was alone, and if someone had a buggy and a baby and some shopping he could only shout:

'You'll have to fold it, you can't leave it there.'

When I was thrown off the bus it didn't come as a surprise that the driver was grumpy. Lots of men hate boys, or so it seems when you're a boy. We often hate the people who remind us of ourselves and our shortcomings.

Certainly none of the teachers at school seemed to like the boys as they pulled hard on the short hairs above our ears, or the ears themselves, or slapped us on the back of the head without warning. Our dads didn't like us, and if we had older brothers they didn't like us either. As for girls, they knew that: 'Findin' a good man, girls, is like findin' a *needle in a haystack*', a song lyric written by two men colluding in the general consensus.

Everyone wanted boys out of their shops, even before we'd stolen anything. There used to be a long-haired hippy who worked at the Pop Inn record store where we bought singles. He was mild and placid (until someone returned a record saying it was scratched, when the problem was their stylus). We saw him once on the top deck of a bus and called out to him, a group of teenage boys smiling and waving from the pavement.

He gave us the finger.

So everyone hates boys but, if you are a boy, the only thing you fear is other boys, chasing you, threatening you and wanting to fight you. Despite all this, if you are a boy and you meet another boy and he says:

'All right?'

Then you must say:

'Yeah, you all right?'

And he'll say:

'Yeah, I'm all right.'

When the lights came up at the end of *Grease* I realised that I'd been sitting a few seats away from my friends. Now under the influence of John Travolta as Danny Zuko, I was affecting a slouchy, slack-jawed gait. One of my mates said:

'What's the matter with you?'

So I gave up that pose before we were through the foyer.

The bus fare to school was 2p when I started at Bancroft's aged ten, the same price as a packet of fruit Polos. A few years later I was a functioning delinquent, vandalising buses with stolen marker pens. Such behaviour in someone bereaved or abused, I'm told, is more positive than a common alternative, depression leading to suicide. Although shoplifting, vandalism and insolence won't earn any accolades for an adolescent, they might be evidence of a person making a space for themselves in the world, having been dealt a poor hand.

From thirteen, Dad gave me the money to go to Arsenal on my own. Taking the number 20 all the way to Walthamstow Central, and then the tube, I wouldn't speak to anyone all day apart from the bus driver and the programme seller.

I'd played alone contentedly as a small child with my mother nearby. Perhaps I carried her with me, so the subconscious feeling was that she was there when I was alone, and being alone felt comforting, even preferable to having company.

I stress that this presence of my mother was a subconscious feeling because when the 55 bus came to the end of its route near my lawyer's office, Mum was not on my mind at all. I thought only about my dad. I had no doubt I wanted to go through with this.

I was admitted through large glass doors by the receptionist who whispered, 'They're already here,' as I came in. I sat down on a square leather seat in the expansive foyer and waited for someone to take me to the meeting room where the police officers were readying their recording equipment. A minute went by, and another. I looked up at the rack of magazines on the wall. There was a handsome man on the cover of one, smartly dressed in a shiny grey suit, striking a dynamic pose. It was an appealing image, but I didn't want to be like him, I didn't want a change of life. I've never not wanted to be me.

Magazines

One day in the early eighties I went to the toilets at Euston station before boarding a train to an Arsenal away game. I was on my own as usual and I noticed some adult magazines on top of a tiled wall, the only time I've seen nudie mags, or dirty books, or whatever you like to call them, in a public convenience. I sidled over to this bounty, a careless pile of glossy periodicals, every cover girl smiling straight at me. They were from the cheaper *Razzle* and *Fiesta* end of the market. As I reached out to turn the pages of the top one a man in a grey suit came towards me. He must have been watching. Seized by a familiar shoplifter's tension, like a schoolboy caught somewhere I shouldn't be, looking at something I shouldn't be looking at, I turned to face the man, distancing myself from the magazines. It was the look on his face that I remember, only that, not the day, month or year, not the journey, just his face.

He was perhaps ten or fifteen years older than me and there was something hopeful in his expression, a plea or an appeal, an open look that told me what he was after. He was a predator masquerading as prey. I didn't know how it was supposed to happen, or how far we would go, but I knew he wanted to have sex and there might be a few quid in it for me.

It was much darker in the cubicles than out in the communal areas, where strip lighting bounced off the floor-to-ceiling white tiles. With no experience, I wasn't sure how much of the transaction took place before you closed that door behind you. He still wore the look, not hostile, though maybe later he'd be horrible, when he'd finished and he wanted rid of me, but he maintained his disarming eye contact, as if he had a white flag in one hand and a hard cock in the other. Is this what Dad did, teenage rent boys? What would I get? Ten, twenty, thirty pounds? I'd never had thirty pounds before. Not all at once.

Even when a man approached me, having piqued my interest with a few judiciously placed top-shelf magazines, a homosexual liaison in his eyes, I still absolutely did not make any connection between this and my father's behaviour at home. Even though I'd called him a 'poof' in front of my family, even though I knew he was sexually aroused by me, I still didn't think he was actually gay. It didn't show in any other part of his life that I saw. I thought it was all just to do with me. That's how it appeared. His was a thorough, careful repression, and I was caught up in it. He gave no clues to anybody else, going as far as marrying, having three children and then marrying again.

I'm not without sympathy for him. There was no possibility of coming out of that closet when he was a teenager. It was commonly believed (still is in some places) that homosexuality is a condition that can be fought with willpower, medication or punishment. The reality of homosexual life in the nineteen forties and fifties was still a fear of imprisonment for indecency and even chemical castration, as inflicted on Alan Turing. This bewildering intolerance towards a particular sexual orientation ran so deep that the prejudice was as ingrained in British society as the Church of England and the class system. For many people, homosexuality simply didn't exist, such was the extent it went unseen. People had lifelong friends who kept their sexuality a secret, as my father did.

When I was at public school in the seventies and early eighties, homosexuality was something to be derided. I once joined my peers as they chased a young lad down the corridors. He'd supposedly been seen kissing a boy at a house party, so we went to find him. Once they had him surrounded, his pursuers didn't know what to do other than taunt and jeer. They wanted him to admit he was 'a poof', giving them licence to do who knows what. He looked terrified, cornered as he was at the top of the steps that went down to the room where all our metal lockers were. There would be no escape were he to be followed in there.

I knew him from primary school, where his mum was the kindly art teacher; he was two or three years younger than me. Now he was cast as prey, tall and slender with big frightened eyes and flushed, hollow cheeks. Unexpectedly, some other boys I knew came to his rescue. One of them spat at us. Among his defenders was a friend I sat next to in geography and it shamed me to be seen on the wrong side of this persecution. Shouts rang around the windowless brick and stone landing. There were no teachers to be seen. Presumably they were all sitting in the fog of cigarette smoke that permanently filled the staffroom. Queer-baiting like this was infrequent only because gay boys at my school did not come out, so it appeared there were none. My role as an acolyte to homophobic bullies was reprehensible.

That it never occurred to me to seek this boy out and apologise reveals my cowardice.

A key indicator of homosexuality for us was if a boy 'got a hard-on' in the changing room after PE. This happened to one tall and effeminate lad who grinned sheepishly in the communal shower while we gathered to mock his thickened cock. On another occasion I thought I'd spotted a swelling among the folds of a boy's towel. When I sounded the alarm, one of the bullies in the year turned on me and told me that I was 'the one looking at it'. The boy I'd tried to humiliate looked at me with pity.

Ironically, I'd been attracted to that particular bully in my first year. He was blond and pretty. I remember showing him some pictures I'd drawn during maths of footballers scoring goals. I was ten, he was twelve, and he looked at me as if I was a time-wasting idiot. Subsequently I incurred his wrath on two separate occasions, both of which finished with him punching me repeatedly in the face. Perhaps he was flirting, but he was too late, I'd moved on. Apart from jumping around my bedroom in the nude with Luke when we were about nine, that was the limit of my homosexual exploration.

The most commonly expressed fear of the homophobe is that a homosexual will pounce on him, most likely when he's bending over in the shower. We knew all the comic lines of the time: 'Backs to the wall, lads' and, 'Don't drop the soap'.

Perhaps the fear had some legitimacy. Many men are rapists after all, ninety per cent of them unreported, but it was the idea that a gay man would *inevitably* constitute a sexual threat that we casually perpetuated.

We pointed out suspected 'benders' to one another by holding up an index finger, like a cricket umpire giving a batsman out, and then folding the middle knuckle so the finger was bent, as in: 'You are bent.' This took hold at primary school, our learned prejudice establishing itself like a virus. Apart from my father's behaviour, which I somehow never lumped in with my burgeoning awareness of homosexuality, the only experience I had of predatory behaviour came in joining in the pursuit of a gay boy, never the other way round.

When I smuggled Dad's home-printed *twink* pictures out of his house in 2017 it was the second time I'd stolen his porn collection, forty years on from the raids on his bedside cupboard. It is impossible to believe that he underwent a personality change brought about by sitting at a home computer, going from an interest in images of young women when in his forties to a collector's obsession with gay teen porn in his seventies. If he'd ever liked any of those *Mayfair* or *Men Only* girls, Meg or Madeline or Elspeth, wouldn't he have looked for them later in life, online? Instead, with doubtless the cheapest equipment he could find, he embarked on the type of printing programme not anticipated by Gutenberg.

The time it must have taken, amid the cacophonous din of whirring inkjets, skating back and forth across sheets of A4 laying down line after line of skin, while the motor jerked the page onwards. What combination of the four cartridges creates a blotchy Caucasian (all the boys were white), and at what cost? A huge quantity of ink went on the hundreds of pictures that were destroyed in the inferno on the lawn. Among those that survived, in Dad's secret folder, I had found a piece of paper from one of the notepads he always had at home. There were two words pencilled on it in his familiar handwriting:

teen boys

Did he have to remind himself what to Ask Jeeves?

Prior to his road-to-Damascus conversion in The New Testament, Saul is on his way to arrest Christians so that they may be persecuted, when he is stopped by a light so bright it leaves him sightless. This lasts for three days, until Jesus, who was dead but arisen so therefore invisible (like an imaginary friend), sends Ananias to heal Saul, which he does even though he doesn't like him.

Something like fish scales fall from Saul's eyes and he can see again.

Ananias subsequently baptises Saul, who then becomes the apostle Paul, supposedly writes half the Bible, and is made the patron saint of London with St Paul's Cathedral named after him, which goes to show you shouldn't be discouraged if you've had a bad start in life.

I mention Saul/Paul in passing only because it was as if the scales fell from my eyes when my stepmother revealed the truth about my dad by handing me a folder of hardcore pornography. Not quite a divine intervention. As I write this so many scales are falling and piling up I suspect if I stop typing and look down I won't be able to see my feet.

How could it never have occurred to me that his behaviour in my room at night revealed his true sexual identity? He molested me frequently, he tried to watch me masturbate, he used to shout 'take your shirt off' when I was in the garden, and he passed no comment on Victoria Principal in *Dallas*, who was so beautiful I became static and silent at the sight of her. He also appeared not to notice Diana Dors or Felicity Kendal or Suzi Quatro or Debbie Harry or Marti Caine or Patti Boulaye or Dana or Pan's People or Legs & Co, or even Selina Scott and Anna Ford on the news, but he couldn't watch Liverpool play on television without referring to their centre half as Alan 'handsome' Hansen, and he could watch Steve McQueen driving in *Bullitt* ALL DAY.

When my stepmother gave me those photographs the realisation came that I had colluded with a child molester over what he did to a little boy four decades ago, when he ran his hands all over his naked body, like a blind man taking in the contours of a living sculpture. If I wasn't going to stick up for that child then I felt sure no one else was.

As the scales fell from my eyes I felt foolish. Of course Dad liked other boys, not just me. It smacks of egomania not to see beyond my own experience and put myself in the context of the wider world.

But then there was no wider world for me; one man decided right and wrong, and used a range of techniques to keep me in place. We almost never had visitors to the house, my brother and I taunted each other in arguments about who had fewer friends, so I struggled to relate to people, to converse, to relax in company, and was convinced no one liked me, perhaps inevitably when living in a house where it appeared no one did. I couldn't put my feelings into words and had no one to talk to anyway. My life folded inwards and I could not see beyond myself. I could only think of a room full of people in terms of what I had to do to prevent them from not liking me, leading to attempts to win favour by bragging about how good I was at something, or relishing being called Brainbox at primary school without realising that no one would really want that nickname, carrying as it does a note of contempt.

Any unlikeable attempts to curry favour made my situation worse. I was off-putting, with a habit of making assertive statements about myself, without noticing anyone else's feelings until it was too late. During one school PE lesson we played basketball for the first and only time. It's a non-contact sport, and being younger didn't matter so much. I passed, caught and dribbled well, able to find space and be constantly involved. I was among the best on the court and it felt great. A couple of my classmates complimented me and asked if I'd played before. So I told them that I was a member of a basketball club, which I wasn't. Their smiles dropped: 'No wonder you're good then,' they said, as if I had an unfair advantage. I had their attention at last and lost it by overplaying my hand. They walked off as I tried to formulate some jokey retraction about beginner's luck.

Being disliked prompted a calming wave of familiarity each time it happened. My psyche determined that I should be isolated in a peer group, never an integral part of it and frequently left out altogether. It was as if I was stuck in egomania, defined as a feeling of personal greatness combined with a lack of recognition, but perhaps it was perpetual bereavement. I had once felt great when I was with my mum, but now her appreciation was long gone and I was penned in a one-man sty. Denied the normal to-and-fro of conversation and of ideas, my formative years were spent in a perverted dictatorship and an intellectual void. I had six years with a loving mother, and after that lived in a dysfunctional environment, with further emotional development coming in fits and starts, if at all.

I'd been naïve, and the realisation that Dad was a despotic predator, not a confused parent, was my Damascene conversion, in that every part of my life can be seen differently now. Of course he fantasised about other boys. I was just the one he could get to and the one he wanted to control. In the meantime, he left out copies of *Men Only* magazine as a heterosexual smokescreen. He ensured that my siblings and relatives were in no doubt that I, and I alone, was the root of all our troubles, a habitual liar and a thief who was so badly behaved he appeared to be using the death of his own mother as an opportunity to make mischief, for reasons no rational person could penetrate.

Now I find myself returning to the Cub and Scout camps Dad went on, and whether he had sexual experiences, either consensual and pleasurable or manipulative and criminal. If he had only been a voyeur, he was noticeably unfazed the night my erection appeared between us. He didn't recoil or even flinch. He was calm and practised in the presence of a hard little penis and carried on caressing me, with a noticeable shortness of breath, before an abrupt exit.

Perhaps he knew I was so embarrassed that I would never tell my siblings. He stood by as my relationships with them first flared up and then rotted, making no attempt to encourage us to get on. The discord suited him since they could be kept on his side, and if I ever piped up that he'd been abusing me, they would be as conditioned to cover for him as I was.

I went from lying in his bed after Mum died, leaving confused love notes in his cupboard, to crawling down to the bottom of my own bed and telling him to go away, and now, when memories of those nights swim back into my mind, as they do every day, I know he won't ever go away, not until I'm dead.

And there'd better not be an Afterlife, with him swanning around and no one any the wiser. That would be hell. But if Mum was there and I went straight over to tell her all about it and she believed me, then that would be heaven, which would be ironic since that's where she was said to have gone and I never quite accepted it.

When my mum died, Dad was no longer in a marriage to a woman evidently his superior in everything but parking the car. Two years later, his own mum died, freeing him from her brand of midget tyranny. It was after both these women were gone, not just from my life but crucially from his, that his abuse of me began. Perhaps his enactment of fantasies was triggered by the grief he felt.

I knew what the man in the toilets at Euston wanted. There was a familiarity in the expression, the angle of approach, the hesitancy combined with a singularity of purpose. But he stopped, his face changed, I wasn't wearing the same look as him, more of a frown that said, I'm just leaving actually and I'll do anything for love but I won't do that.

Maybe it was a mistake, he was young-ish, good-looking-ish, I may have denied myself the best blowjob of my life, or him the worst of his. Now he looked a little afraid and awkward. I walked past him, through the turnstiles and up into the station.

I knew he wasn't coming over to join me in looking at the men's magazines. It was clear those were both an enticement and a camouflage, a necessary heterosexual front in that place, but only now do I consider my father's bedside magazine collection to be similarly both a lure and a deception. Only now I know the truth of his lust for boys do I realise that my abuse wasn't about me, no more than it would be about me if I disturbed a wasp nest and they attacked. I was in the wrong place (desirable suburb of a great city in the first world) at the wrong time (just after the invention of Angel Delight).

Those were jokes. I meant the wrong place (my bedroom) at the wrong time (the night).

Jokes

I was in an aisle seat so there was a chance I'd be noticed, but we were quite far back. I was practised at putting my hand up: 'Me, me, pick me, I'll get it right, somebody *praise me*!' But this wasn't school; it wasn't Mrs Thorogood I was signalling to. The cute little girl in front of me also had her hand up. Was I looming over her like Donald Trump behind Hillary Clinton in a TV debate? It was obvious they'd choose this replica Shirley Temple ahead of me. I looked around, every child in the place was volunteering. I tried to find another centimetre of fingertip. A man from the show had come down into the audience and was approaching us; who would he choose? Hillary or Donald?

He picked us both! We were rushed up to the promised land of the stage. There we turned to face the audience, the lights were bright, I couldn't see anything or hear what was going on, it was hot and my instinct was to find cover like exposed prey. Instead, I faked a smile and hid my fear. There were about eight boys and girls and none of us knew what was happening: 'Who cares? *I'm on stage!*' Maybe it was a pantomime, I can't remember: '*Who cares? I'm on stage!*' But I think it was an old-fashioned Scout Gang Show, an amateur revue: '*Who cares? I'm on STAGE!*'

The man who chose us asked the first boy a question. I couldn't hear his answer but the audience laughed. Was he funny? Would they like him more than me? I could just make out that each kid in the line was being asked to say:

Supercalifragilisticexpialidocious.

I could hardly believe my luck, that's from *Mary Poppins.* She's the motherless child's ideal woman. I knew *all* the songs. I was infused with the confidence of someone certain they're about to excel. When it was my turn, almost before being asked, I said:

'SUPERCALIFRAGILISTICEXPIALIDOCIOUS!'

I awaited my applause. The man was looking at my face but it was as if he couldn't see me. The audience murmured and clapped a bit. I'd played the Brainbox card, what an idiot. Was I that smart-arse no one likes? '*Who cares? I'm on stage!*' The man had moved on to Temple, and she said: 'Thooperfwabadosh . . .' and then gave up, didn't even get to the end, useless, missed out several syllables and messed up the ones she tried. I smiled pityingly. It wasn't her fault, she was only little, like my sister. The man should have said: 'That was *rubbish,* do it again!' But the people were laughing. He did ask her to do it again and she didn't say it right once, if anything she got worse, but the applause, and the laughter! The audience appeared to be unanimous: girls are just wonderful, they're hopeless and stupid but so pretty and adorable it doesn't matter. We love them for their unthreatening vulnerability and their willingness to smile when the world finds their efforts laughable. Unlike that *boy* over there with the fake smile who got it *right,* what's he so happy about? *Prick.*

I walked back to our seats with the girl, so everyone could see us together, but she broke into a run and it looked

like I was chasing her down. We'd both been given tubes
of sweets. I reached forward in my seat to give her some of
mine. She then gave me some of hers, and I gave her more
of mine. 'You were fantastic,' I said, though I was aware
that I was overdoing it, just to keep the euphoria going. Her
accompanying adult glanced at me and my dad told me to
stop. It was over, my personal high point of the nineteen
seventies. But can they take away the memory? No. Nor
can they extinguish the joy we brought to so many.

The urge to get on stage then lay dormant for years, until
a family holiday to Corfu when I was thirteen. A traditional
Greek dinner was laid on for tourists with bouzouki music,
funny waiters and plate smashing. I soon decided there is
nothing better in life than a Greek taverna, and that one
day I'd visit Greece again. After the food came the dancing,
with everyone invited to join in. Some women at a nearby
table who had been enjoying themselves all night ('That's
the wine laughing,' said Dad) were already up. The waiters
came over to us: 'No, thank you,' said Dad, with no eye contact. My brother and sister stayed put but I faked a smile,
hid my fear, and joined in. I soon had my arms across the
shoulders of some drunk strangers, and their arms across
mine, while the music began with a menacing air as if this
was just a taxi to the runway. We had to cross our legs one
way then the other as the whole circle speeded up, there
was broken crockery everywhere, and just when we were
all laughing and holding each other up, a man appeared
taking photographs.

On stage, everyone laughing, and photos too? Heaven.

The next morning I imagine a few people missed breakfast, and a van must have turned up with new plates, but
most importantly, dozens of photographs from the night

before were pinned up and on sale. I found two of me in the midst of the throng but Dad wouldn't pay for them. I felt rebuked, as if I'd shown him up.

Three years later, after leaving school, I began a Media Studies course at Loughton College. There I found a place where the thrill of going up on stage, and of impromptu dancing in a taverna, could become my daily bread. Drama classes! I would never have signed up for them but they were part of my course. I went on to a Drama degree at the University of Kent where I spent four years acting in plays and trying comedy. By the time I graduated I decided again to fake a smile, hide my fear, and be a stand-up comedian.

I was twenty-two at my first gigs, but I looked about the same age as I had in Corfu. Casting around for ideas for material (on the London comedy circuit you wrote your own stuff, no old gags, nothing stolen), I came up with a routine about the Bayeux tapestry, which ended with me lying down in front of the audience. Later I had another about cycling and another about the Grand National and another about smoking on aeroplanes, all of which ended with me on the floor. It's unusual for a comedian to lie down, no one else was doing it, but perhaps no one else made their mother laugh, when they were three, by lying on the floor waving their legs in the air like windscreen wipers. I only now realise how similar I must have looked, twenty years on, prostrate on little comedy-club stages in rooms over pubs.

One of my peers remarked, with characteristic perspicacity, that when he saw me on the floor he'd found it 'a bit sad'. I was wounded by that remark but I couldn't see what he meant, and my routines continued to go down well. I didn't make the connection with the past until I began writing this book.

Another comedian I knew, who'd also lost his mum at six, believed he'd always been seeking his mother's love in the form of the adoration of the audience. We'd both been doing stand-up for over ten years by then, but when he asked me if I felt the same way I just didn't think that applied to me. But who else would indulge you, smile at you and laugh on cue, for ten, twenty, thirty minutes or longer, while you fool around in front of them? Only an audience member in a comedy club or your mum; no one else could stomach that degree of need.

I thought I'd just been lucky to discover I had an aptitude for comedy, the origins of which can only really be guessed at. But perhaps the fuel to try stand-up, something many people dread the thought of, came from the need to give a voice to the happy little boy I was with my mother. Whatever it was that started me off, I now had a platform, to be heard, listened to, and above all not ignored. Again, it's only now that I realise that was exactly what I'd always craved.

There's little evidence that Mum was quick to laugh, but I was willing to work for her approval. My Uncle Geoff said that if she went into the Scout hut and her Cubs were charging around she would shout '*Pack*' and they would immediately line up in silence. Uncle Pat's daughters, my cousins, told me that they were frightened of Mum. When I was a baby and they were small children, they wanted to hold me but were afraid to ask her, even though she willingly let them.

I don't remember Mum ever being cross with me, and all the playfulness that I honed in her company probably surfaced as an asset in stand-up comedy. But a comedian needs other qualities, anger being one. Even the silliest of the great comedians I watched, like Robin Williams or Richard Pryor, had an unmistakable angry streak. Laurel and Hardy were constantly dropping things on each other's toes or slapping one another.

Fortunately, I was angry, so much so that in my late teens I hit every member of my family. I had developed such a resentment of authority it seemed unlikely I could hold a normal job for long. Consequently I had no money, which was a great motivation for trying to get paid gigs in comedy clubs. Dad once told me that he didn't enjoy his National Service in the RAF (despite his love of Spitfires) because he didn't like being told what to do, another taxing inheritance.

But rage is a good tool for a comedian, as deployed by Dave Allen, and exemplified by Sam Kinison, or by the equally inimitable Gerry Sadowitz, who specialises in savage contempt for anything in sight.

Early in 1989 I was on a bill with Sadowitz at the Tunnel Club in South London. When the microphone didn't work he picked up the stand, threw it across the stage and shouted his whole act over raucous laughter, bemoaning politically correct restrictions on language before justifying his favourite phrase on the grounds that: 'You fucking cunt is an onomatopoeic classic.'

Earlier in the show my comparatively tame set had defused the wrath of the Tunnel's notorious hecklers and I was still carrying some residual adrenalin when Sadowitz came over. 'You'll be on TV in five fucking minutes,' he said, which I took as a thrilling compliment, 'children's fucking ITV.' He chuckled to show he was teasing and turned back to the pool table, where he displayed startling hand-eye coordination. I later discovered that his close-up magic show is the best you will ever see, particularly if you admire creative swearing.

I was no Sadowitz but I had anger from my dad and playfulness from my mum, two key components in an identikit comedian. There is a third crucial quality, though, and that is a tolerance of humiliation.

The nerves I experienced at early gigs were similar to those when I was shoplifting. But I was virtually immune to shame. Nothing could ever be as embarrassing as being thirteen years old, stark naked, with my erection buried in my father's stomach as he writhed against me in his underpants. I think about that incident every day despite it being over forty years ago. No other single moment in my life comes back to me in the same way. My capacity for surviving humiliation and embarrassment is considerable, to the extent that I sometimes wonder if my subconscious seeks it out as a familiar and therefore comforting state.

I went on holiday to Majorca, with two boys from school, when I was sixteen. There was a group of nine women from Newcastle in the hotel. They were in their twenties, all laughed continuously, and tolerated our beginners' attempts to have sex with them. One of them had a black one-piece swimming costume, which I put on and then went down to the pool. Her friends were laughing but one of mine could not cope. He felt ashamed, as if it was happening to him.

'What are you *doing?*' he said.

'Sunbathing.'

'You look ridiculous.'

It was true, I did.

'No, I don't.'

'Take it off,' he said.

No one was laughing any more. He was the same boy who used to punch me in the face at school so I backed down, but only after I'd posed for a photo, which I still have.

In conclusion, as a comedian I was a Triple Threat:

1. Childish.
2. Angry.
3. Shameless.

In 1989 I was a runner-up in the *City Limits* New Act of The Year competition at the Hackney Empire. A television producer gave me her card, and told me about her show, *First Exposure,* which offered new comedians a spot on TV. A few months later I was back at the Empire in front of the cameras.

For the recording I bought a red polo shirt, which I paired with the navy blue trousers I'd worn at my graduation the previous summer. I looked like one of the golfers on the public course in Chingford, where that exact outfit was mandatory, and where my dad had started playing as part of his plan to get into his brother's golf club.

Arthur Smith, the show's compere, introduced me:

'He's got a very silly name, but a very funny act, please welcome Alan Balgonie.'

Arthur knew me by my real name, but Equity had told me they already had an Alan Davies so I had to choose a stage name for the TV. Mum's maiden name was out, since Alan Price was a famous musician, so I took the name of the street in Chingford where I was born, Balgonie Road. I didn't use it for long; Arthur had rightly put me off. I went back to my own name and after a few years the union relented.

When I walked out at the Empire, the faded old Music Hall auditorium was lit up and looked magnificent, beautiful; it was exhilarating to be up there. I went over to the microphone, which I dared not take out of its stand because my hands were shaking, and spoke terrifically quickly about dolphins being trained to plant bombs in order to rescue laboratory animals caged for vivisection. I recorded the show on a VHS tape. It's here somewhere.

Dad was in the theatre. Afterwards he said:

'You're wearing my golf shirt.'

'It's not your golf shirt, I bought it from Next.'

'It's my golf shirt.'

'No, it isn't.'

'Why didn't you use the Davies name? It's our name, the Davies name.'

'I'm not allowed to.'

'What?'

'I'm not allowed to by Equity.'

He evidently thought that ridiculous and that I was mistaken.

'Arthur Smith is funny, isn't he?' he said.

'Yes, very, he's the best compere on the circuit.'

'I liked him, he was very funny,' and then he said 'Arfur Smiff', in a bad cockney accent. We didn't talk about the dolphins. I remembered his displeasure a few years before when I'd plastered my bedroom walls with anti-vivisection posters featuring caged animals in experiments, replacing pictures of all the members of Adam and the Ants. As I sat on the bed I'd been abused in as a boy, behind a closed bedroom door, looking up at all these photographs of trapped creatures suffering in silence I failed to identify the roots of my empathy and compassion for them.

The week after *First Exposure* Dad bought me a red T-shirt and asked me for his golf shirt back. It took my sister to convince him he was wrong.

That summer I took my fledgling act and my golf shirt to fringe festivals in Canada, starting in Winnipeg, then taking in Edmonton, Vancouver and Victoria. In October I returned home wearing a money belt stuffed with Canadian dollars and with a solid twenty-minute set that would work not just in Manitoba and Alberta, but in all the new comedy clubs that were springing up in London.

I returned to Loughton with my backpack to find no one home. Without house keys I had to climb over the side gate, pull a ladder out of the garage and climb into my brother's bedroom. That night I heard Dad complaining to my stepmother about my breaking in, as if they had security issues to address. When he heard about the dollars in my belt he told me I needed to start paying my way and to give him some money, and that I should do more around the house.

'You need to try to be part of this family,' he said.

It evidently wasn't in his vision of the future that I'd be back at home after university. The year before I went to do my degree I'd had a physical fight with him, just before I turned seventeen. I'd come home late, we'd argued, he took a swing at me, and I punched him in the stomach. Good times. I left the next morning.

My drama teacher from college, Piers, lent me his flat in Forest Gate for a week as he was going away. He just gave me the keys. I'm still grateful. Years later I discovered he ran a comedy club and he gave me my first paid gig (£9). When he died his wife wrote to say he was 'so proud of you' and that email still brings tears to my eyes.

While I was in Forest Gate I went to Newham Council

housing department to ask for a flat. A man in a grey suit asked me if I *could* go home and I said yes and that was that. Even if I'd said my dad used to come into my room at night, I doubt it would have made any difference. As it was, that didn't occur to me. I went back home after a week because I had no money. Dad had put a new stereo in my room. I hated it.

That was six years before, in 1983, and now here I was clambering back through a window. If there was an antonym for the prodigal son, I was it. I exchanged my dollars for pounds, bought a copy of *Loot* and began to look for a room to rent. Before I left I wrote my dad a letter. I said it wasn't true that I did nothing around the house. I was the only one who did his own washing and made his own meals, and that I had tried in the past to be a member of the family but that:

'I was rewarded with sexual abuse.'

I left the letter on top of the chest of drawers in his bedroom, along with some cash. He never acknowledged receiving it. I found a room in a house in Stoke Newington and moved out just before Christmas, with a new decade about to begin.

Dad next came to see one of my gigs in 1994 at the Lyric Theatre on Shaftesbury Avenue. The show was to be recorded for release on both video *and* audio cassette, with the imaginative title: *Alan Davies – Live at the Lyric*. Dad told me he'd like to come but I asked him to stay away for fear of being distracted. He bought a ticket and snuck in. Perhaps he was just curious, or perhaps he was terrified about what I might say. He needn't have worried. Though I lampooned his 'dad-size pants', I did so without mentioning that whenever I thought of him wearing them I remembered being naked with his hands on me. I mocked his dating tips, about the risk of girls falling downstairs, without knowing that he was obsessed with teenage boys. I knew my autobiographical tales only scratched the surface of my life but I was enjoying myself. I was the delighted recipient of a Critics Award for Comedy at the Edinburgh Festival, I hosted a weekly Radio 1 show with a brilliant cast of comedians and I had the lead role in a series on Channel 4. In 1996 I was cast as the eponymous hero in David Renwick's *Jonathan Creek*, which ran for twenty years and aired to millions on BBC1 in the slot once occupied by *Dallas*.

I was famous, which had always appealed to me.

I loved working as a comedian and actor throughout the nineties, but by the end of the decade I said to my agent, by way of a cry for help, that I was only happy when I was on stage. 'That's very sad,' he said, 'let's book you in for some gigs in December, there's nothing in the diary.'

In 2000 I moved into a huge apartment in a converted match factory near Highbury Fields, with its own indoor swimming pool and a roof terrace overlooking London. I had all the supposed trappings of success. That Christmas I sat on a giant suede sofa, alone, for six days, without speaking to anyone at all. Then I threw a New Year's Eve party and drank champagne in my pool in a kind of parody of happiness, acted out in front of everyone I could think to invite.

Soon after that I stopped doing stand-up. In my mind the comedy clubs had changed, now it seemed everyone knew who I was. I felt I couldn't muck around and wing it on stage as I once did. And I stayed away from it for ten years, which was a mistake. Audiences just want you to be in control and make them laugh. Losing that outlet for expression, and the grounding camaraderie of my peers, was disastrous. I became paranoid, I didn't trust anyone. I even left my agent, who I began to suspect was ripping me off and I never, as a deliberate policy, answered the phone or the front doorbell.

I needed to address all those memories and emotions that I couldn't work through in stand-up or anywhere else. Eventually, I enrolled on a Creative Writing MA at Goldsmiths College and, after several months there, anonymously submitted a piece I'd written called *Hands*. It felt like a breakthrough, as if, at last, I had my emotional head above water. A few weeks later I was shown my father's porn collection and I went back under.

Submissions

After my interview with the police, in which I reported my father's crimes of the nineteen seventies, I waited sixteen months for the outcome. Then, in February 2019, while I was sitting on a beach in Jamaica, watching my youngest child paddling at the water's edge, my mobile rang showing a UK number. I surprised myself by answering it, and heard a voice I didn't immediately recognise. Frowning behind my prescription sunglasses (that are too big and make me look like Susan Sarandon), I asked warily who was on the other end. It was my lawyer calling from her office on Hanover Square.

Had I realised it was almost five o'clock on a Friday afternoon in cold, dark London town, then I'd have known she had some news for me, since they do go in for those last-thing-on-a-Friday calls in the legal profession. And she did, at last, have some news for me.

Over a year earlier, my lawyer had sent Dad's favourite pictures to the Internet Watch Foundation, which was set up to scrutinise online child pornography in an effort to protect minors. This was after I'd driven around Essex paranoid about being discovered with all this potentially illegal material, eventually hiding it in my car overnight. The IWF had concluded that the images were not prosecutable. None of the boys were evidently pre-pubescent and it could not be proved that any of them were under eighteen. Although it seemed apparent that many were in their early teens, it was possible they were chosen because they looked young. This meant downloading and viewing the images did not constitute an offence and that Dad's pornography could not be introduced as evidence of his character in any case relating to his abuse of me, since he was not looking at those pictures at that time. They went into storage at my lawyer's office, where they remain. Any case against my father would depend on the interview I gave to the police.

Meanwhile, my stepmother told me over the phone that she could tell my dad had been looking for the pictures. It was clear that he had not been told I had them and he was probably not going to be confronted at home. She did tell me once that she had said to him: 'You'd better not have done anything to Alan,' but that he'd just walked out of the room and slammed the door behind him. She tried again on another occasion and he said: 'I didn't really do anything wrong, I just bathed him.'

It had never occurred to me that something else was going on during Sunday bath times, where he soaped my torso with bars of Lifebuoy, washed my hair for ages and then dried me. As I write this I'm trying to keep the memory of my mother in the front of my mind, as she put me in that same bath with my socks on and we laughed together. Let that be my lasting memory of that bathroom, not a new sordid insight; socks & laughter, socks & laughter, socks & laughter, socks & laughter. Hopefully that will do it.

So in October 2017 my lawyer had set up a meeting with the police at her offices and I had boarded the 55 bus and gone to be interviewed.

The detectives I met were experienced. One was a middle-aged white man with the air of a thin-lipped thief-taker, who looked a Scotch and a cigarette away from a part in *The Sweeney*. His colleague led the questioning while he remained impassive, apart from a slight shake of his head when he learned my brother had not been in touch after he found out Dad had molested me.

My brother has subsequently responded to my revelations in his own way. He no longer sends birthday cards to my children.

The police asked whether my siblings had also been abused. I said I didn't know but that my sister had told me she wasn't, and that she'd asked my brother and he'd said that he wasn't either.

I worried, during the interview, that the wiry, inscrutable detective resented schlepping across town to meet this other middle-aged man in the type of well-appointed meeting room rarely seen in the public sector. That was my fear at least, stemming from my own uncertainty in coming forward, and not from anything the police said.

The senior officer had a kindly demeanour, and twenty-nine years on the force, many of them specialising in sexual assault cases. The majority were rapes of women, where traumatised and physically harmed victims are coaxed into giving evidence, with every chance they will later be vigorously challenged on the veracity of their accounts. Conviction rates for rape are extremely low, which discourages victims to speak up, as does the fear that it will feel as though they are on trial as much as the accused, should they ever go to court. Less than ten per cent of rapes in the UK are reported, and the criminal justice system routinely fails known victims of sexual assault, partly because it is difficult to secure convictions. The unknowable statistic is the number of victims who tell no one.

The senior detective told me that offenders sometimes present outright denial combined with attempts to discredit the accuser, but on other occasions abusers were relieved and unburdened themselves, as the interview became a confessional.

I said I didn't think that would happen in this case.

I was told to take my time, and ask for a break if needed. It had been suggested I come with someone to the interview, or have someone waiting for me afterwards (I hadn't and I didn't), since going through unpleasant past events could be upsetting and a victim ought not to relive the experience before going back out into the street as if nothing had happened. I'd often dealt with things alone throughout my life, and it had taken me so long to come to the decision to speak up that I believed I would be able to cope. My lawyer was in the next room too.

My abuse, without penetration, restraint or physical harm, was not difficult for me to recount once I'd arrived at the decision to do so. Breaking free of my father's strong psychological influence to tell the truth had been my struggle, made easier because of the feeling engendered in me by my close friends that I could and would be believed.

The detective complimented me after the interview and I had the oddly inappropriate feeling that I'd done well, such is my weakness for praise. But I had been achingly sad on that 55 bus on the way there, sitting up against a window on the top deck, just remembering. I walked close to buildings for weeks before and after the interview, again occupying the smallest space I could in the world, avoiding eye contact and dreading being asked: 'How are you?' since I would struggle to say: 'I'm fine, how are you?' as convention demands.

Soon after that day the senior detective rang to say my dad had been interviewed. I almost wished I could have seen him wrestling with his misogyny as he was confronted by her, and with his racism, since she was black.

'I've had a very difficult afternoon with your father,' she said.

I think I replied: 'Haven't we all?'

She told me he had not wanted to be interviewed. He'd resisted vigorously, claiming he was too unwell to be questioned and that he couldn't remember things. She'd had to persist and he'd tried to be charming and she'd seen a little of how he might work on people to soften them and persuade them, but he did, eventually, have to answer her questions.

He denied all wrongdoing, or that any such events had occurred at all, but despite that, tellingly, he let slip my name in the interview before he'd been told it was me making the complaint. Even so, when she asked him about being confronted in that airport departure lounge in 1981 by his son calling him 'a poof' and saying he came into his room at night, he had replied:

'That was a very good holiday.'

She had concerns about his short-term memory but could see that his long-term memory was good. In common with many Alzheimer's patients it was, if anything, becoming better. She and the thief-taker set off to investigate any possible instances of abuse of children while my dad was involved in the Scouting movement.

My stepmother was also going to be interviewed. She had previously expressed concern about two elderly brothers who had turned up unannounced on the doorstep wanting to reminisce with my dad about being in the Scouts together. She thought they might intend to extort money over historical sex abuse. It was the appearance of these two men that had caused her to break the seal on my father's sexuality and give me the photos. She was the only one who knew that he liked teen-boy pornography and she wondered if he'd abused these two men when they were boys. Perhaps she could believe it because she knew that, before they were married and under the same roof, Dad used to come into my room at night. I'd mentioned it to her many years before, after she had said, perhaps cryptically:

'If I'd known what your father was like, I never would have married him.'

She first raised her fears about these two elderly men to my sister, who she then told all about Dad's pornographic pictures and how they'd secretly burnt hundreds of them in the garden, and how she knew he still had some, and then my sister called me and said, with a curious echo of Max Bygraves:

'I wanna tell you a story.'

The *twinks* were thereby revealed to me, shedding new light on Dad's night-time visits to my bedroom, and immediately after that came a further revelation from my stepmother that our dad had once had a sexually transmitted disease, some twenty-five years earlier. At the time she'd moved out of his bed into the spare room, with a portable television and a Yorkshire terrier, and had chosen to live like that permanently, rather than leave.

My sister and I speculated briefly on where Dad had

picked up the infection, and after quiet reflection, the only phrase that fits is:

'God knows.'

It's likely that Dad knows, since twenty-five years puts the occasion firmly in the long-term memory bank. Meanwhile, my stepmother stayed with him, as a masochist to his sadist. I don't know what she told the detectives when they interviewed her but they concluded that she wanted out, that she might soon 'vote with her feet' and leave. I told the police that I had asked her: 'If you were in a flat of your own and my dad was in prison, would that be a better life for you?' and she had said 'yes', so I had offered to help her financially but she'd stayed put.

The investigations into my dad's time with the Scouts in the forties and fifties came to nothing. The Scout Association has been dogged for decades with allegations of child abuse. One firm of solicitors online even provides an interactive map of the UK marked with locations of sexual abuse by one hundred and eighty sex offenders connected to the Scouting movement. A similar map exists for the US. A successful outcome for many of these solicitors is not to secure a conviction but financial compensation, for which there is a time limit. For abuse in childhood the claim has to be made within three years after the victim's eighteenth birthday. The Scout Association has insurance in place for such claims. Many historical complaints are probably lost.

Perhaps Dad always hoped to live a conventional married life after the Scouts. There are no stories of him having any other girlfriends or of Mum having any other boyfriends and I don't know if she knew about him, if she noticed his eye drifting to teenage boys, or why she waited five years for him to propose. They found each other for whatever personal reasons and they began a new chapter of their lives and had nine years of marriage and three children and then she died.

As the investigation continued, Dad's home computer was taken away. It was old and sometimes it broke down and one day the person who fixed it for him said that he was no longer prepared to do the job and never came back. The police told me there were tens of thousands of images of boys posing nude or having sex with each other on there, but not pre-pubescent boys so therefore, despite several images described as borderline, it was not possible to prove they were below the age of consent and nor was it possible to convict him for looking at these pictures, since down-loading, retaining and viewing them does not constitute an offence, exactly as it was with the printed pictures in the PG Tips bag that I had nearly shared with that peloton out in the Essex countryside.

Despite finding no other victims, the police still believed they had a case, and that my dad was a criminal. So they prepared their evidence and went to the Crown Prosecution Service.

In June 2018, a year after I was handed the porn collection and eight months after I was interviewed, my lawyer received a letter from the CPS saying they were not intend-ing to prosecute my father, as they didn't think they would be able to convince a jury that what he'd done to me con-stituted sexual assault.

The offences were committed in the seventies and would have to be tried under the legislation, from the fif-ties, that was in force at the time and which they said was inadequate to secure a conviction based on my account. I needed to have had some genital abuse or forced penetra-tion to be considered harmed by what had happened to me.

I was disappointed with this outcome, partly because it appeared to vindicate my siblings' view that the police would not 'do anything' because of our father's age and medical condition. I knew that the police very much wanted to do something. It's not for them to decide whether his health would affect a decision to prosecute. They told me they'd previously gone into a hospital ward to find a suspect.

My lawyer was infuriated. It was as if I'd been sent away for making a fuss about nothing. She told me I was entitled to ask for a more detailed explanation of the decision and so it was arranged that two lawyers from the CPS would meet us in the same meeting room where I'd first spoken to the police. The one deputed to explain the outcome was a slim, young woman in a dark fitted jacket. She pulled her laptop out of a coloured computer case, as she might have done as an undergraduate, possibly not so long ago. Her voice was shaky. The second lawyer, a grave middle-aged man, in need of a good meal, sat alongside her as back-up. I felt like my case was part of her training.

I was told that the CPS has a two-part process to go through when deciding whether to proceed. Firstly, the evidential requirement: is there enough evidence to convict? Only if that threshold is met do they move on to the second part: the public interest requirement. They then consider whether the person they might successfully prosecute is a danger to the public, or is likely to re-offend, or whether they are fit to stand trial.

They said my case had fallen at the evidential hurdle and that they had not considered whether or not my dad was fit to go to court.

The young woman said that, because I'd told the police in my interview that I believed my dad had always wanted it to look like he was just cuddling his son, a jury might, in fact, be persuaded that's what had been happening. I'd always considered that this would be his escape, a version of events in which he was being affectionate, and with just my word against his I would never be believed.

Furthermore, she said, because I'd mentioned that after my hard cock had poked him in the tummy (not her words), my father had stopped stripping me off, then a jury might conclude he'd realised the effect he was having on me and had immediately desisted. They might be persuaded that it was never his intention to arouse me or for there to be any sexual element to his affection for me.

I asked whether they thought that, if they were defending my father in this case, they could get him off? They smiled and said yes, and I smiled ruefully and thanked them for their time and they smiled again and shook hands and left. I looked down from the window as they crossed the road outside and watched the young woman as she walked away, and thought about the engagement ring on her finger and wondered about her fiancé, as she went out of sight behind a building with her suited chaperone.

What caught my father's eye when he was out in the world? A smartly dressed young woman or only teenage boys with their shirts off playing cricket or jumping in a pond, or whatever they do at Scout camp? Or was it just me who had piqued his curiosity?

My lawyer suggested that I might be very disappointed with what we'd heard from the CPS. I said that I was, given that the only evidence in the whole case was my interview, and that they had said repeatedly that my story was compelling and credible, so for it to be turned against me was a shock. It was absurd to suggest that my father was demonstrating normal parental affection. It would be unthinkable for me to go into my own children's bedrooms to strip them naked and caress them. Dad had told me not to 'tell anyone about this cuddle', after all. He was evidently gaining sexual gratification from what he was doing. I could tell by his breathing, by his interest in my buttocks, by the unnatural silence in the room, that this was a type of sex.

The law was baffling to me. People can find themselves in serious trouble for verbal harassment and abuse or vile messages, or any unwanted attention that creates discomfort or acute embarrassment or is intimidatory. Why is this man not in trouble for stripping a boy naked and molesting him? His own son, in his own bed, shortly after he lost his mother, so there was no one he could tell.

The local review within the CPS had upheld their decision, but my lawyer said I was entitled to pursue my case under the Victims' Right to Review Scheme (VRR) and it would cost me nothing. The CPS may, she warned me, still conclude that they wouldn't prosecute. It was highly unusual for them to change their minds. Despairingly I wondered how it could be any different. There was no new evidence. It felt like the end of the road. He could lie and deny his way to the grave.

Then my lawyer said we could hire 'counsel to make submissions', at a cost of about £6,000. We talked about leaving no stone unturned and going back to the CPS to say they'd mistaken child molestation for normal parental affection and the damage to me had been lifelong.

So we hired a barrister who asked for a transcript of my original interview with the police. This took two months to arrive, and in October 2018, while I was away filming for the BBC in Glasgow, I was asked by my lawyer to make time for a conference call. I could only do this on my mobile during my lunch hour, while wearing a costume that included false teeth, a prosthetic face and a hunchback. We managed just a forty-five-minute call with counsel, but that was all she needed. When I was back at home in London a few weeks later, I received a nine-page document.

Referring to several legal precedents, counsel showed that where an assault is inherently indecent, in other words where an incident had occurred that 'right-minded persons would clearly think was indecent', then 'there is no need separately to demonstrate an intention to commit an indecent assault'.

Whatever the protestations of innocence that would be made in defence of my father, it is possible *to infer wicked intention from the facts found proved as to the circumstances of the assault* (which is a phrase that I considered as the title of this book).

The important thing is that my evidence was found by the CPS to be 'credible and compelling'. In other words, a jury would likely believe me, not just because I'd said it in my police interview but also because I'd raised it before to many people, including my dad. His own barrister would still have to contend with my evidence even if his client was stuck in 'it was a lovely holiday' mode.

As the document went on it became clear that Dad's interest in my bottom was not going unnoticed. It had been stated, in the judgment of another case, that acts of assault need not be 'overtly sexual' but 'may only have sexual undertones'. Several other cases were cited where the stroking of thighs and buttocks without consent, even through clothing, can be considered sexual assault.

Counsel set out the conduct of my father that would be considered inherently indecent:

1. Taking my clothes off when there was no need
    to be naked.
2. Touching intimate places, including the buttocks.
3. Referring to special cuddles, and acknowledging
    that this was abnormal.
4. Keeping the touching secret and always only
    doing it when we were alone.
5. Ignoring my humiliation and my attempts to
    avoid the touching by hiding under the covers.
6. Taking sexual gratification from the touching.

The document went on to say that the touching of genitals is not a prerequisite to indecency and that the fact
that Dad stopped stripping me after the incident when I
became erect does not mean that it was not an indecent
assault. It also concludes that my mother's death is not rel-
evant as a defence. There is no extra attention being paid
to me because Dad was concerned about that loss and the
bereavement we had suffered. The molestation began years
after she died and ended a full seven years or more later.

As I write this I try to picture Mum reading the document,
sitting on the sofa in my front room close to where I am
now, as if she had been brought back into my life somehow,
after nearly fifty years. Would I show it to her? Would she
be surprised that Dad was capable of these things? Would
she be most upset about that, or to learn of the splintered
relations between her children?

Perhaps I'd take her to the Old Vic first, or a matinee
at the new Globe Theatre for some familiar Shakespeare.
From there, by the Thames, would the new buildings, like
The Gherkin and The Shard, or the Globe itself, astound

her? Afterwards I'd take her to meet my children when they came home from school. Would she think my two boys look just like me, as many people have told them?

When my sister met our Auntie Hazel and Granny Price at Adelaide Airport in 1988 she was nineteen years old, and Granny kept saying:

'Doesn't she look like Shirley?'

'Yes,' said Hazel.

'*Doesn't* she look like Shirley?'

'Yes, Mum, she does,' said Hazel again, as we walked to her car in the heat of the day.

If my mum were here, on my sofa, would she ask about them, her mum and her sister? And her dad?

'They're all dead, Mum,' I'd have to say.

'And what about your dad?'

'He's got Alzheimer's.'

'What's Alzheimer's?'

'You dodged a bullet there, Mum.'

I might remind her of a time she and I were at home in Loughton with her mum, my Granny Price. Perhaps it was 1970. They were talking about my dad. I was listening but not understanding, absorbing who knows what, as toddlers do. I decided to make a contribution to the conversation, since I'd been quiet for a while. Adopting the tone they used, I said:

'What time's Roy coming home?'

They looked confused at first, and then they smiled.

'What time's Daddy coming home?' I said, correcting myself. They were laughing, which put me off trying to join in like that again, although they seemed to find me endearing, and Mummy said:

'Later, dear.'

It was apparent they hadn't finished all they had to say about Dad. I couldn't understand any of it so I went back to playing nearby. While she's here I'd like to ask Mum if she remembers that, but I know that if I turn my head to look I'll see she's not on my sofa. I don't need that physical confirmation that I'm on my own, that she's only in my mind, so I'll carry on tapping at this keyboard. She is here somewhere; I hesitate to say she's in my heart because it's not a term I'd ever use. I also don't look at the stars above and imagine that one of them is Mum. And I've never previously imagined her nearby, physically, a whole person reading thoughtfully, and then speaking to me as one adult to another.

If I *could* show her the CPS document I'd be pleased, perhaps, for her to see that the barrister's submissions concluded the original CPS decision was flawed for two reasons:

1. It failed to recognise that a right-minded person would consider that stripping a child naked, stroking and caressing their body, in particular their buttocks, in secret, is inherently indecent.
2. Even if it is not inherently indecent, it is capable of being indecent and was in this case. My credible and compelling evidence demonstrates that Dad must have intended to commit indecent assault.

After I'd read the document it was as if two people had put my arms over their shoulders and were taking my weight, so I would not psychologically sink to my knees and stay there. It seemed things were now ninety-to-ten in my favour, even though I still felt my dad would never tell the truth, that he would always lie, to the point where I wondered if he really believed he'd never done anything wrong.

My lawyer delivered our submissions to the CPS and we waited. I was told I would have a response during November 2018, then in early December, then definitely on December 21st, timing that would spoil someone's Christmas, but then January 2019 came and went with another promised deadline passed.

My lawyer assured me this was a good sign; my submissions were being taken seriously. The CPS had been in contact with the police, had a transcript made of my interview, and were asking a specialist prosecutor to look into the case. It seemed they might prosecute my dad, that we'd be in court with everything laid before a jury, and I became anxious about the actual day, imagining my family there, or rather *his* family. Where would everyone sit, on whose side?

I knew, of course, they'd all sit with him. If they didn't he'd behave as if he'd been betrayed. Even though they know he is a child molester, it would be too hard for my siblings and stepmother to shake him off. He'd make them feel terrible about it, whereas I have been unable to engender the same feelings in them, even as the adult representative of a boy they once knew who was abused and traumatised by his father.

My wife would come to court with me, and perhaps some of the friends I'd confided in, if they could. Maybe my cousins would come, Uncle Pat's daughters, who had listened to my story and offered support in a compassionate and understated way reminiscent of their father, though it would be difficult for them as it is their dad's brother on the other side.

A couple of friends had asked me if I was concerned

about media interest in this story. Despite the anonymity granted to victims in these cases (and the heavy penalties associated with breaches of that in the press), the accused has no anonymity and, with the internet appearing as lawless as the Wild West, there was a risk of the case being reported on, particularly if it went against me. How would I feel about that intrusion?

My answer was that a person who wants the victim to be quiet is on the side of the abuser. Mine wants me to be quiet, and all other abusers would also want me to be quiet, in case their victims take a lead from my speaking up and raise their hands and confide to their friends, and possibly to the police, and realise the shame is not theirs to carry.

I dreaded court, facing him, knowing how powerful the urge to comply with his desire for secrecy had always been over the years, how my siblings wanted it all kept under wraps, thinking he would be dead soon. That his control would only stop when his heart did.

Sitting here writing (no imaginary friend on the sofa now) I remember an incident only yesterday when I was alone in the living room of my home and I knew there was someone in the hall outside the door about to come in, either my wife or one of my three small children. There was a tightening in my chest, a flutter of anxiety, like scar tissue flaring, the Post Traumatic Stress Disorder that can be traced back to my fear at night, in my bedroom, that he would come through the door, even though he usually didn't. The unease was constant, and that is the deep, cumulative, lifelong effect of living with your abuser.

For fifteen years in my twenties and thirties I lived alone, and for many of them I smoked cannabis every day, believing this to be a lifestyle choice, not a consequence of past events. I would drink white wine at the same time and play hundreds of hours of repetitive video games, like *Tomb Raider*, *Formula One* and *FIFA* (*97*, *98*, *99*, etc.). In that numbness, with the deadening marijuana, the sweet-tasting alcohol, amid the drip, drip, drip of tiny rewards in the games (with an avatar of myself scoring goals for Arsenal), I could slip into a trance-like state of separation from the outside world that, a psychotherapist helped me to understand, took me towards the blissful peace I'd known when breastfeeding. But in health terms this behaviour was going to kill me, not strengthen me like my mother's milk. It was not helping me to grow, it was fixing me in time and soon the clock would begin to turn back slowly to zero.

I believed that I was breastfed not because of any first-hand account or photographic evidence, as is now commonplace, but rather because as a boy I used to suck my thumb and rub my index finger against the side of my nose. When a toddler does that the finger replicates the feeling of the mother's breast against their little face. It seemed that my taste for the numbing effects of alcohol was rooted in infancy and that, although I could cope with being on my own, as I had somehow internalised my mother (having passed many hours contentedly alone with her), there were other difficulties in my adult life and in the face of those I would try to go back to the earliest memory of Mum, a sense memory, an unconscious recollection.

There was a temptation to return to those behaviours, rather than think about my dad in court, but after a while the handful of friends I had confided in, always individually in a quiet corner of a restaurant somewhere, started to express their strong support, and anger. Emails and text messages began to arrive, once they'd had some time alone with what they'd heard from me. Most of them said they had been in tears thinking of that little boy without his mummy, with this man controlling and abusing him, breaking his trust and inflicting emotional and psychological damage, and they wanted him punished.

'I hope they get him,' they said, in different ways, at different times: 'I hope they get the bastard.'

My youngest was filling his bucket with seawater and pouring it into a hole I'd dug for him in the sand, and it was a blissful moment, nourishing for my health and happiness, just to see him pottering around and talking to some imaginary friend or other, and then my phone rang and it was my lawyer calling to tell me that she'd received a document from the CPS and to remind me that it was almost unheard of for them to change their minds and overturn a decision, extremely rare, something they don't really like to do.

And she told me they had changed their minds and reversed their original decision, having taken our submissions into account. My story had been believed in part because it was full of failings of memory, uncertainty about dates and times and the frequency of the abuse, but consistently clear on what he did to me, and how he'd told me to not tell anyone, though that was only the first time, after which it was understood.

The CPS decided I'd suffered a serious breach of trust and repeated instances of sexual assault. Were my father charged he'd likely go to prison to serve between six and twenty-four months, probably twelve. I thanked my lawyer and she said I would need to go to see her in London when I was back.

There was still the issue of whether it would be in the public interest to prosecute.

Doctors

My father's leg was visible under the covers from where I sat at the end of the bed. It was just the two of us in the quiet, sterile room. I couldn't see out of the run of windows high up to my right and there were no sounds coming from outside the bedroom door. He reclined on his pillows.

The bedclothes covering him had been tented to form a triangular tunnel, which allowed air to circulate around his grotesquely swollen leg and prevented the sheet sticking to the continually oozing discharge that coated the skin in a clear glaze. I glanced at it from time to time.

We talked about the ongoing rugby tournament in France. England had just beaten the hosts in the semi-finals of the 2007 World Cup. I'd made a recording of that match, and their earlier win over Australia, and brought a portable DVD player for him to watch them on.

I asked if there was anything he needed and he said he'd run out of underpants. I could see into the en-suite bathroom where a washing line held a few pairs of drying Y-fronts. It was apparent that he was wetting the bed. Understandably, he said he only wanted Marks & Spencer underwear and that I'd be sure to find a branch somewhere, which I did later on without even looking, when I emerged into the centre of Athens on an escalator from the Metro to find M&S directly in front of me. It felt, briefly, like someone was helping me.

He folded up the copy of the *Daily Mail* that I'd brought him on my second trip over the week before. I couldn't find his usual *Telegraph* and the *Mail* was all they had at the stand by the Syntagma metro station. He appeared to have consumed it from cover to cover.

'That was a really good read,' he said.

'Was it?' I said.

'Yes,' he said, his smile dropping.

I didn't have a paper for him this time. The flight from London to Greece was four hours but trekking from the city centre out to the Athens equivalent of the North Circular had been the worst part of the journey on my previous two visits, so I was in a hotel in Kifissia, a nice suburb much closer to the Hygeia hospital, but less tourist friendly with no English newspapers to hand.

Two whispering nurses came in. They didn't come near either of us. As soon as they were in earshot Dad asked me if I wanted some tea. I said I didn't.

'Could we have some tea?'

It was evident that they had no English so he upped the volume a bit.

'*Tea?*'

Blank looks.

'A cup of TEA?'

They left. I suspected they knew what he wanted.

'You wouldn't have to ask in England, would you?' he said. 'Wouldn't have to *ask*.'

The nurses came back, without tea, and then five doctors came in, all wearing unbuttoned white coats.

I'd seen them before. The one lurking at the back, who never spoke, was the surgeon who would cut off Dad's leg, should the infection spread into his bones and overpower, from that stronghold, the intravenous antibiotics that had been pumped into him for three weeks. As usual, I tried and failed to make eye contact with The Sawman. They had exhausted everything bar surgery and he might be reaching for his toolbox this very day depending on the imminent update.

The doctor at the head of the group started speaking. She was a handsome, middle-aged Greek who, with tanned skin and an expensive-looking haircut, bore solemnity and authority in equal measure. Deploying both of these qualities, she explained in perfect English that the infection had been turned around, the most recent MRI scan (for which Dad had to: 'lie *completely* still for *forty-five* minutes') had shown that it was receding.

This was more hopeful than the earlier prognosis of certain amputation and possibly death. They left and I never saw them again.

'I like her,' said Dad. 'She speaks very good English.'

'Yes,' I said.

'She trained in America, you know,' he said.

I imagined her telling him that after he'd asked why her English was so good, by way of a rebuke to the others.

A few years before this Hellenic crisis, the offending leg had been bitten by a snake on Theydon Bois golf course, in Essex. My Auntie Carol, who, like Uncle Pat, was a longstanding member, went to ask the groundsman if there were adders in the long rough.

'Oh yes,' he said, 'they've been reintroduced.'

Dad had shown the two puncture marks just above the

top of his shoe to my stepsister who was a GP. She said it was not a snakebite, probably just a scratch from a bramble. A week later he was in hospital, his lower leg swollen like a rugby ball and black as coal from knee to foot.

The entire limb remained permanently vulnerable to infection and now, while it was submerged in the Mediterranean, some waterborne pathogen had found a break in the skin. Initially he was hospitalised on the small Greek island that he and my stepmother were staying on, but he was soon airlifted to Athens. I spoke to my stepsister on the phone.

'I saved your dad's life,' she said, 'I told them he should go to a bigger hospital.'

My stepmother had returned home from Greece, my brother and sister did not visit him and he was there alone, elderly, scared, and urinating the moment he nodded off.

While I was trying to show him how to make the DVD player work, the phone by his bed rang. It was my sister. They spoke for a couple of minutes and then he hung up.

'She's ever so caring, isn't she?'

'Yes,' I said.

'Ever so caring.'

Silence.

'I don't like to keep her on the phone for too long. She has the boys.'

'Yes,' I said.

He looked up.

'So you're going sightseeing today, are you, having a little holiday?'

'No,' I said. 'I've been to Athens before, for the Olympics, I'm here to see you.'

And when the time came to take him home I escorted

him to the airport as he bickered with the nurse sent by the insurance company.

'I'm glad you're here,' she said. 'I'm finding your father quite difficult.'

I said he was probably embarrassed, since he was carrying a colostomy pouch in a Tesco carrier bag, but then he complained when he asked her for a ham sandwich and the only one she could find also had cheese in it and he opened it up and peeled out the slice of cheese and handed it to her, all the while pulling faces as if she was feeding him a cat-shit baguette.

At check-in three seats had been booked for him to keep his leg up during the flight but they were on the wrong side of the aisle, so I argued with the staff and they swapped them around with a scowl. At Gatwick, I helped him into the private ambulance his insurance company had sent to take him round the M25 to home. He shook hands with me from his wheelchair and said thank you and was staring out with weary trepidation when the door slid shut.

Back at home he was fending off attempts by my step-mother to persuade him to agree to sell the house and downsize. He was seventy-four and appeared frail. He would never play golf again. All he wanted, he said, was to sit in his armchair, looking out at the garden that was easier to see now that the magnolia by the patio had gone. I left him in that chair imagining he would soon die there, not that he would head upstairs to click on *print* hundreds more times, before climbing up on a stool and stashing piles of porn high up in his built-in wardrobe.

When my father was diagnosed with Alzheimer's he imagined the same descent into amnesia and irrational behaviour, often in The Middle Of The Night, that his brother Pat had suffered. He feared the future. I felt sorry for him and said that as long as he wanted to stay in that armchair and look out at that garden I would support him.

The porn remained a secret, his abuse of me seemed a distant deviation. He had been grateful for my assistance when he'd been at death's door. It's apparent that I was still trying to please him and win his favour in my adult life.

It was only when his shrunken brain had sunk him into the fog of dementia that my stepmother told me the truth about her collusion with him to conceal his true nature. It was that discovery that prompted a complete reappraisal of my life under the control of an exploitative, sometimes violent, sometimes self-pitying, authority figure who would never apologise or admit he was wrong. The cumulative effect I have come to understand is a traumatising subjugation. He is a narcissist, gripped with self-loathing for his repressed latent homosexual desires. He has little capacity for empathy or sympathy. His principal concern when my mother was dying was the impact on his life, so he controlled what she knew, what her sister knew and what his children knew. When he was sexually abusing me he cared only that he should not be found out, and that I must not be believed in any event.

But I was believed. In overturning their ruling, the CPS had affirmed my story. Not only that I had been living with a child molester, but that I had challenged that person about what he'd done and spoken of it with family members and friends and healthcare professionals over many years. This wasn't something I was only now making up.

The CPS were persuaded that what he had done was worthy of a custodial sentence, that, in their words, he had 'an interest in you that was sexual and not paternal'. He was a criminal, a child molester, who should be on the sex offenders register.

But he had recently been declared unfit to drive, not just because his silver BMW had unexplained dents all over it, but because he couldn't find his way home from places he'd been going to and from for decades. My stepmother and brother had taken power of attorney over his affairs, which would make it much harder to convince the judge that Dad was fit to plead.

The accused must be able to follow the day-to-day business of the court. At the outset of a trial my dad's barrister would attempt to demonstrate that his client was not fit. Then both prosecution and defence teams would have him examined by doctors. Given the debilitating nature of his condition, and that he would be at least eighty-six by then, it seemed likely that he would be declared not fit to plead and that, even if he was, minimal sentencing would apply.

The most likely outcome would be an absolute discharge.

As I read and reread the last of the thirteen pages in the CPS review of my case, it sank in that they weren't going to do it, there would be no trial. With the help of my stepmother, he had kept his lust for boys a secret and left me unable to see the truth about him until he was too addled to be held to account.

He'd got away with it.

Throughout the years of abuse he'd tried to maintain, in the words of the CPS review, 'plausible deniability', by dressing up his undressing of me as paternal love. This felt like a controlled and deliberate ploy, which ultimately only succeeded because of his medical condition. Though I wonder if, were it possible, he would have taken a year in prison and the destruction of his personal reputation in exchange for a decade or more with Alzheimer's.

Despite this outcome I realised I had what I needed. The document from the CPS said they believed me, not him, which means that all those who have covered for him and protected him and failed to challenge him for years can now know they sided with a child molester against his own son, who is the victim of crime. There would be no trial, and no waiting for a trial either, and that was a relief.

In among the information supplied by the police and detailed in the CPS report, reference was made to a letter from 14/11/89 'in which you directly accuse the suspect'.

I was astonished. That was referring to the handwritten note I'd left when I was twenty-three, in which I reminded him of his past sexual abuse of me. Although he never acknowledged receiving the letter, he'd kept it, for nearly thirty years. Whether the police found it or it was handed to them I don't know, but his hanging on to it for all that time feels like a guilty conscience at work. Or was it a souvenir? The police still have it on file.

A few months further into 2019, my stepmother had to go into hospital for an operation and, with no one to care for him, my dad went into a home. While he was there he immediately stopped soiling the sheets every night, which he'd been doing for years. My stepmother had cleaned them every day, to save his embarrassment. But it turned out, consciously or otherwise, it was not an accident but a ploy, to create a secret between them that she wouldn't want to reveal, to keep her in that house with him, albeit in the spare room. But when she came out of hospital it was apparent that she could no longer care for him, she needed someone to look after her, aged eighty-five with various ailments including the onset of dementia. My brother visited the house, sat in his father's armchair and told my stepmother that all Dad wanted was to sit there and watch sport on the television. But she said no, she couldn't manage any more, it would be better if he stayed in the home. And no, she didn't want to visit him just yet.

Cards

In March 2018 I received a birthday card from my father. He hadn't sent me one for years. The assumption was that he couldn't remember anything due to his Alzheimer's. So for a card to arrive was a little disturbing, especially since the police had told him not to contact me while he was being investigated.

He had denied all wrongdoing in his conduct when I was a boy but now, in this small gesture, was he putting a hand out to me? He was eighty-four at the time.

There was nothing in the card that hinted at that, though, just a characteristically bland sentiment scribbled down in that familiar handwriting that I hadn't seen since the slip of paper with 'teen boys' written on it had appeared, when I was sitting in my car going through his porn the previous summer.

The card was of the type he would give me when I was young. They always seemed to have a generic image of a game of football, rugby or cricket on them. Others featured cars, aeroplanes or, as in this case, steam locomotives, and were doubtless the sort he'd received himself as a boy.

It was as if Dad was thinking of the little boy he'd abused. That was the person in his mind's eye that he was sending a card to. Not his grown-up son who was turning fifty-two and had reported him to the police less than six months previously. Was this an effect of the Alzheimer's? Was he confused? I was on his mind, but on his mind in my child-hood, which would be all too clear in his intact long-term memory. Perhaps he hoped this card might function as he believed buying me a stereo would in 1983, by persuading me to soften my position and come home.

Could it really have had even a trace of manipulation in it? This was how he'd operated in the past. Was he think-ing: 'He's not happy, this could develop badly for me, I'll send him something.'

Was he trying to say a tiny sorry to the little boy?

Where had he managed to find an old-fashioned card like this? A drawing of a big green steam engine travelling through what appeared to be England's green and pleasant land, but very much designed to appeal to a child (a boy, of course). How he loved steam trains, referring frequently when I was young to *Mallard*, the famous engine from his childhood that set the world speed record for locomotives.

Did the card tell me that he knew full well that he'd been interviewed, that the boy he abused had finally said something? Was it meant to prompt the boy to start visiting again so we can all go back to pretending it didn't happen? Or was I just in his mind for reasons he couldn't articulate or recall in his condition?

But I'd seen the porn collection by then, and knew that steam trains were a thing of the past for him, he wasn't into them any more and hadn't mentioned *Mallard* for years. This card isn't the kind of picture he likes these days, it's another piece to be added to a concealing col-lage that's been created over a lifetime. Another little fragment of falsehood, which is now in the hands of the Metropolitan Police.

It only served to make me think again of the boy I had been, and of the boys in my father's favourite pictures, and how I'd considered releasing them from my sunroof to flutter across the Essex countryside. Perhaps the folder would have opened in my hand, the pictures caught by the air as the car raced along, first one or two, then a flurry of them as if they were being freed.

All those boys back out in the world, if only they could land in the fields and somehow come alive in contact with the earth, stepping out of the pictures to say their names and where they are from, and how old they were at the time, and maybe recall who the photographer was, and in saying those things immediately forget them, then walk down into Loughton and far beyond, to wherever home is, eventually absorbed back into life, into school, with no online past, returning to their youth, their childhood, like lost wartime pilots emerging still young from the Bermuda Triangle.

My hope for them is that they would be believed.

As I hope all boys with a story to tell will be believed, not just those in a grim pornographic photo shoot from the past, but those boys held by an internal grip of the mind, that originates in some private and awful series of events that have an unseen but lasting effect on their lives, and possibly on their children's lives. A grip that remains hidden because they always thought they'd never be believed, in the face of a powerful adversary masquerading as someone who cared for them, who is prepared to deny everything, as if nothing could be more ridiculous than the idea that they are an abuser, an exploiter, a manipulator of children. The hope is that one day that grip might be loosened, perhaps as one story is told so another might emerge, attached like links in a chain being pulled out of the sea. A man might look an old friend in the eye with something in his expression unlike anything that's previously passed between them, and say, on behalf of the boy he once was:

'I'm going to tell you something now I've never mentioned before and all I ask is that you believe me.'

When I first conceived of writing my story I would imagine 'Dear Mum' at the top of page one, to help me write without thinking these pages would ever be read. I used to want her to know what had transpired after she'd left. I didn't manage to begin that letter and in the end my efforts to tell the truth (as if my hand were on the old book half written by Saul) mean the pages have been written by me and for me, as much as anyone. Memory is so elusive and mine has surprised me time and again. Decades of distance combined with bereavement and trauma can make a mockery of simple recollection, so the story is necessarily incomplete but wholly truthful.

As is expected in memoir some names have been changed to protect the innocent, some left out to protect the guilty, and vice versa. Some were put in and then taken out again, as to see them on the page made the writing too difficult to carry on with. Some are real but may seem made up, like the thoroughly good Mrs Thorogood.

Above all, I have set out to tell you the things you don't know about me, in the hope that, one day perhaps, you will feel able to tell someone what they don't know about you.

Acknowledgements

I am grateful to many people for helping me with this book.

Initially it was anonymous feedback on an assessment at Goldsmiths that encouraged me to go beyond 'why would anyone want to read this?' I was tutored there by the wise Ardashir Vakil: 'We write to discover the things we do not know about ourselves,' he said, 'not just to set down that which we already know.' I nodded and avoided eye contact. Only during my work on this book did I understand what he meant. He also suggested I write as if 'no one is looking over your shoulder', which is hard, and to write 'the things that make you cry' which I did. Thanks, Ardu.

I was also privileged to be taught by Francis Spufford, whose perspicacity, humour and apparent knowledge of everything ever written was joyous.

Pam Johnson gave me rigorous tutorials for two years and then took time to read pages and provide invaluable advice long after the course was over.

It was in Blake Morrison's Life Writing group that some chapters from this book were hatched and then discussed by Blake and my fellow students, Caolan Blaney, Sylvia Saunders, Helen Longstreth, Kate Richards and Nina

Reece. Thank you to all of them for compassion, criticism and confidentiality in equal measure.

After Goldsmiths I found support in trusted readers, none more so than friends from my time at the University of Kent in the 1980s, Mandy Martinez, whose enthusiasm, notes and proof reading were hugely appreciated and Jackie Clune who provided so much encouragement. Thank you.

Thanks also to Oliver Scott, Morwenna Banks and Tom Connolly for taking the time to read and for considerate and insightful comments.

Thank you to Maureen Vincent for introducing me to Robert Kirby at United Agents, who understood what I was doing straight away and thanks to him for introducing me to Susannah Waters, whose editing of my first draft was alarmingly thorough, led to many extra hours of work and was exactly what I needed. Thanks to Richard Beswick and Zoe Hood at Little, Brown for your sensitivity and guidance.

Finally thank you to my wife Katie who has read every word and listened to all the fretting and worrying, and the padding around downstairs early in the morning (it was 5am when I got up to write this bit). She saw all the staring out of the window and experienced much general irritability, and as for what I was like when I began to write, well, you can imagine.

Katie and I are lucky to have a daughter and two sons, who might read this in time, when they will learn that watching them as they grew up helped me to see myself differently when I was a child, to better remember, and to reassess, and inspired me to stick up for that boy and, in so doing, other children too.